JOB MATTERS

HOLZTECHNIK

von
Thomas Ryan

unter Mitarbeit von Roland Reiter
und der Verlagsredaktion

Cornelsen

How to use the book

Job Matters Holztechnik ist ein modernes Lehrwerk für den Englischunterricht.

So finden Sie sich im Buch zurecht:

Zu Beginn jeder der 24 Units finden Sie eine Übersicht über die Themen, Fertigkeiten und Grammatikbereiche, mit denen Sie sich anschließend eingehend beschäftigen werden.

IT'S YOUR TURN

Die ***It's your turn***-Aufgaben am Ende jeder Unit stellen einen zusammenfassenden Abschluss der Unit dar und richten sich an diejenigen, die gezielt an weiterführenden sprachlichen Fertigkeiten arbeiten möchten. Hier können zudem eigene Erfahrungen der Lernenden eingebracht werden.

ICH KANN

	Seite/Übung
☐ Ich kann eine Rolle in einem Dialog oder einer Simulation übernehmen (z.B. in Berufssituationen). A2/9	11/4c

Nach jeder vierten Unit greifen ***Extra practice***-Seiten das Gelernte noch einmal auf und bieten so ein zusätzliches Übungsangebot zu den Themen der vorherigen Units. Außerdem zeigen Ihnen ***Can-do-Statements***, welche Fertigkeiten aus dem Gemeinsamen Europäischen Referenzrahmen für Sprachen bzw. aus dem Europäischen Sprachenportfolio Sie in den Units erworben oder gefestigt haben.

Für heterogene Klassen werden innerhalb der Unit differenzierte Aufgaben angeboten und durch Sterne gekennzeichnet (★ = leicht, ★★ = mittel, ★★★ = schwer).

I would like to work in/at/for …	because it is a creative environment.
	because I like films / the theatre / timber factories.
	because I would like to work outside/inside.
I would like to work	abroad / in Germany because …
I would not like to work in	any of these environments because …

Praxisbezogene Redewendungen und Phrasen finden Sie in den grünen Kästen.

Weitere wichtige Symbole:

2 = kennzeichnet Höraufgaben und gibt die entsprechende Tonspur an. Die Hörbeispiele sind separat als Download (ISBN 9783064513235) erhältlich unter www.cornelsen.de.

= kennzeichnet Tipps und wichtige Hinweise

Viel Spaß beim Lernen und gutes Gelingen wünschen Ihnen die Autoren und der Verlag!

Contents

1 Your career

This unit is about:
- career opportunities
- activities

Competences:
- listening to a radio interview
- writing about your future career aims
- discussing career options
- describing a carpenter's tasks

2 1 Becoming successful in the timber technology sector

Peter Young owns a huge carpentry firm in London. In a radio interview, he is talking about becoming successful in the timber technology sector.

★ a) Listen to the recording and then complete the dialogue.

Shutterstock / Monkey Business Images

Interviewer: In today's show, *Professional Life*, we are talking to Peter Young, an owner of a successful carpentry business, about the secret of his success. Hello Peter, welcome to our show.

Peter: Hello, thanks for having me.

Interviewer: What can you tell us about working in the wood technology sector?

Peter: I believe that the carpentry business is the ideal career opportunity for c_reate_ [1] young people. G_ood_ [2] carpenters provide a wide range of useful services. A carpenter is responsible for constructing and maintaining residences and buildings. This includes building items such as furniture and stairs, making repairs to the internal and external structure and ensuring buildings are safe. A t_alent_ [3] carpenter has e_xcent_ [4] manual skills and a good technical understanding. You need to know the most r_ecent_ [5] developments in wood technology and come up with u_setul_ [6] ideas. If you are a responsible person and interested in technology, this could be your dream job.

★★ b) Work with a partner. Describe what a successful carpenter does. Make a list of useful vocabulary and present it in class.

2 Career options

In the carpentry sector, you will be able to work in a wide range of professional environments.

★ a) Look at the words below and match them with the pictures.

film and theatre sets • ~~timber factory~~ • ~~housing~~ • furniture construction • public property (e.g. schools, hospitals) • repair and maintenance

1

Shutterstock / Irina Mos

housing

2

Shutterstock / Dmitry Kalinovsky

____

3

Shutterstock / Aleph Studio

timber factory

Shutterstock / Cynthia Farmer

public property

Shutterstock / Istvan Csak

film and theatre sets

Shutterstock / Tom Tom

furniture construction

★★ b) Discuss with a partner. Which of these areas would you like to work in? Can you think of any others? The phrases in the box will help you.

I would like to work in/at/for …	because it is a creative environment.
	because I like films / the theatre / timber factories.
	because I would like to work outside/inside.
I would like to work	abroad / in Germany because …
I would not like to work in	any of these environments because …

★★★ c) Write down five sentences explaining which of these areas you would prefer and why.

3 A carpenter's tasks

There is more to working in the wood technology sector than just manual work. Look at the list of tasks below and then tick the tasks carpenters often perform.

- [x] lifting and pulling heavy objects
- [x] building stairs and other items
- [ ] writing newsletters
- [x] operating carpentry tools and equipment
- [x] calculating
- [x] checking emails
- [x] helping with small tasks
- [x] taking phone orders
- [x] making measurements and selecting materials
- [ ] welding
- [ ] putting up scaffolding
- [ ] calling the police
- [ ] using a cash register
- [x] maintaining tools and equipment

4 Career aims

★ a) What are your career aims? Use phrases from the box or your own ideas to form sentences.

> finish my apprenticeship • work for a large building firm / carpentry firm • have my own carpentry business • be successful in my job

★★ b) Discuss the following questions in class and take notes.

1 Why do you and your colleagues want to work in the timber technology sector?
2 What are your career aims?

★★★ c) Write down five sentences about your colleagues' future plans.

> **IT'S YOUR TURN**
> Think about your everyday experiences in the workplace. Make a mind map about your daily routine in your job.

2 Tree growth

This unit is about:
- the life of a tree
- parts of a tree
- the forest
- types of wood

Competences:
- describing a tree
- labelling parts of a tree
- listening to a recording
- talking about wood

1 The life of a tree

Read the following description of the life of a tree and label the pictures below with the words in orange.

The tree begins life as a seed. It germinates into a seedling.
This grows into a sapling, which is then transplanted into a forest.

1 
____

2 
____

3 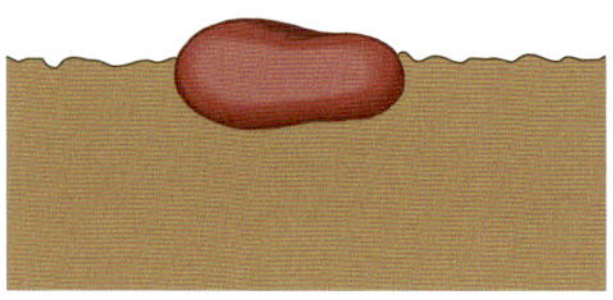
____

4 

____

2 Parts of a tree

A tree consists of many different parts. Complete this text with words from the diagram.

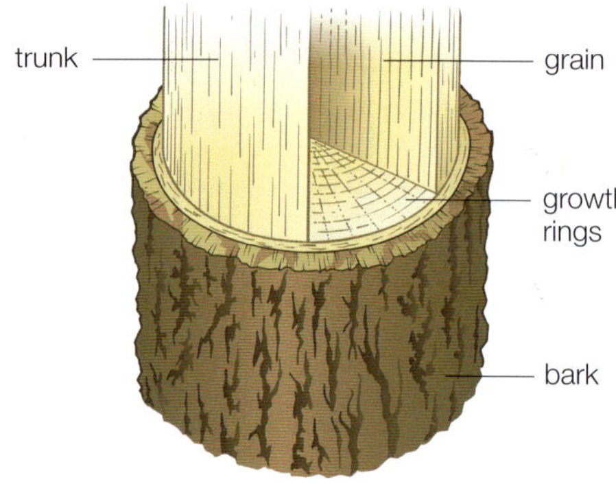

We get most of our wood from the __________[1] of the tree.

The rough __________[2] protects the growing wood.

The age of a tree can be estimated by counting the number of annual

______________[3].

These will form the ________[4] in the final product: timber.

3 🎧

3 The forest

Listen to the recording of the manager of a sawmill talking to a visitor. What does the sawmill produce?

A When the sawmill cuts the trees into logs there are four by-products:

1 ____________________ 2 ____________________

3 ____________________ for gardens 4 ____________________ for animal bedding

B Logs are made into two main products:

1 ____________________ 2 ____________________

4 Types of wood

Wood can be classified as hardwood and softwood. Different types of wood are used for different kinds of furniture.

★ a) Work with a partner and decide which is the most suitable type of wood for the products below.

window frame

fishing boat

garden furniture

toy

tool handle

dining table

book case

interior door

coffee table

gate

external door

stairs

Type of wood	Class	Uses
oak	hardwood	
pine	softwood	
teak	hardwood	
ash	hardwood	
larch	softwood	

★★ b) Work with a partner to complete the role-play.

Apprentice	Skilled carpenter
What can I make with …?	Well, … is suitable for …
I want to make a/an/some … What type of timber should I use?	For that you'll need a hardwood/softwood. You could use …
Can I use … to make …?	Yes, that's OK. *or* No, that isn't suitable. Try … instead.

IT'S YOUR TURN

Work with a partner. Go on the Internet and find pictures of and information about different types of timber and how you can use them. Prepare a poster and present it in class.

3 Felling and conversion

This unit is about:	Competences:
• timber in the forest • cutting the timber • types of timber • trades	• writing about timber in the forest • describing types of timber • listening to a recording • writing about trades

1 Timber in the forest

What does a forester do? Complete the text with words from the box.

chainsaw • elephants • horses • logs • sawmill • trees

Shutterstock / Muellek Josef

A forester selects __________ [1] for harvesting. Trees are usually cut down with a __________ [2]. Then all the branches are cut off. The trees are now called __________ [3]. In some countries they are then pulled out of the forest by __________ [4]. In some Asian countries __________ [5] are used to pull them out of the jungle. These hardworking animals are cheaper than big machines and they don't damage other trees or the ground. The logs are usually pulled to the nearest river and floated down to the nearest __________ [6].

2 Cutting the timber

There are different ways of cutting timber. Match the diagrams with the descriptions.

Tip	
warp	sich verziehen
grain patterns	Maserung
shrink	verkleinern
swell	quellen

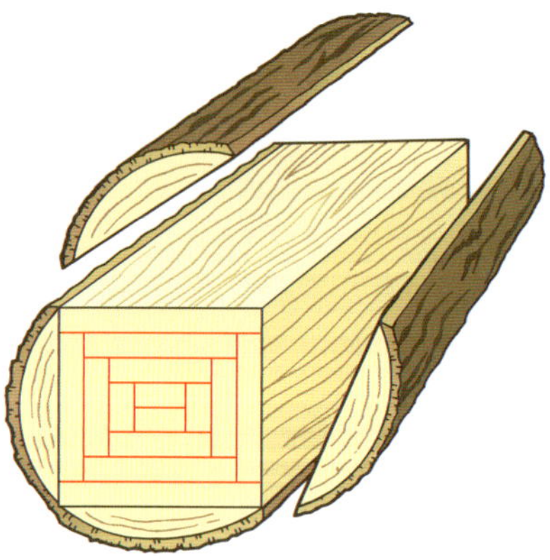
A tangential sawn

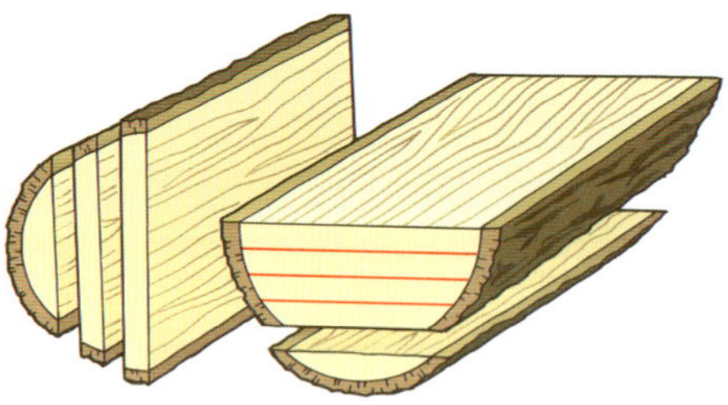
B plain sawn

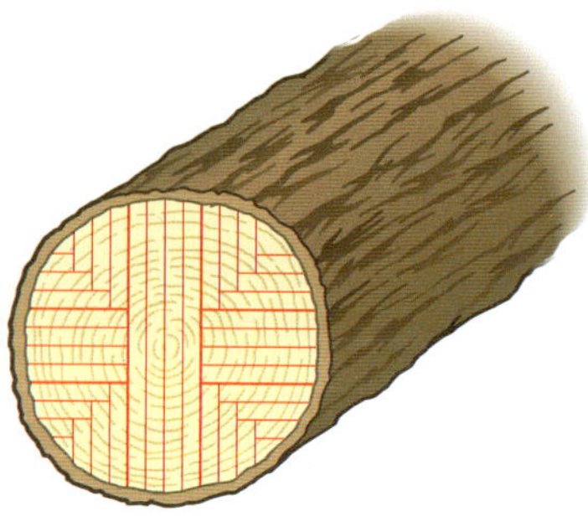
C quarter sawn

1 This is the cheapest method of cutting the log but planks cut this way shrink unevenly and often warp. Then they can only be used for rough work. ___

2 This method means that the log must be turned often. The process takes longer and is therefore more expensive. The planks often swell and shrink easily. ___

3 This method gives the best quality timber. It has good grain patterns and can be used for high-quality woodwork. ___

3 Types of timber

Peter Young's carpentry firm has received a new delivery of different types of timber.
Label the illustrations with words from the box below.

batten • tongue-and-groove floorboard • moulding • plank • skirting board

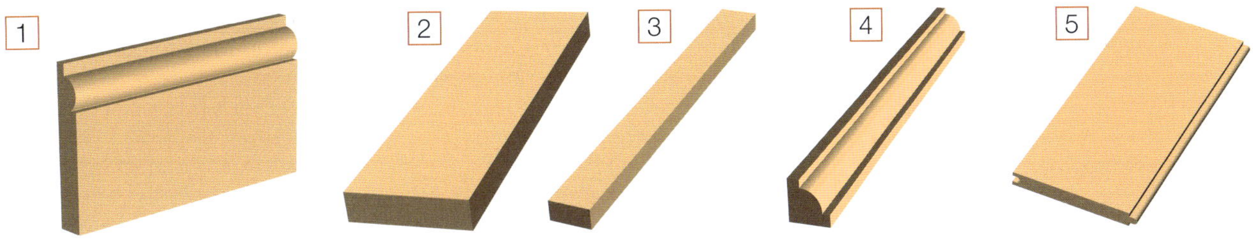

1 ________ 2 ________ 3 ________ 4 ________ 5 ________

4

4 The timber supplier

Listen to the recording of an apprentice talking to a timber merchant and take notes. Then complete these sentences using words from the box.

1 Planks are often used for ________.
2 Planks are also used as floor ________ when extra strength is needed.
3 The ________ are used to secure roof tiles.
4 Battens are nailed to the ________.
5 Most floorboards have ________ and ________.
6 The floorboards here are made from good quality ________.
7 Floorboards can be ________ and varnished for a good finish.
8 Skirting boards are examples of ________ boards.
9 Some of the materials are smooth and some are very ________.
10 The rough materials come straight from the ________.
11 The smooth materials are more ________.

battens
expensive
grooves
joists
moulded
pine
rafters
rough
sanded
sawmill
scaffolding
tongues

5 Different trades

A lot of different people are involved in the process of cutting and manufacturing timber. Use words from the box to complete these sentences.

driver • forester • lumberjack • machinist

1 The ________ identifies the trees that can be felled.
2 The ________ cuts the trees down.
3 The tractor ________ moves the logs out of the forest.
4 The ________ operates the saws that cut the timber.

Fotolia.com / Kletr

IT'S YOUR TURN

Work in pairs. Take turns to describe the advantages and disadvantages of the different methods of cutting timber mentioned in this unit to your partner. Then write a fact sheet about the different methods.

4 Manufactured boards

This unit is about:
- board production
- board types
- waste timber

Competences:
- writing about board production
- discussing waste timber and its use
- listening to a recording about different types of timber

1 Board production

Here is a description of board production. Study the illustrations and then complete the text below with words from the illustrations.

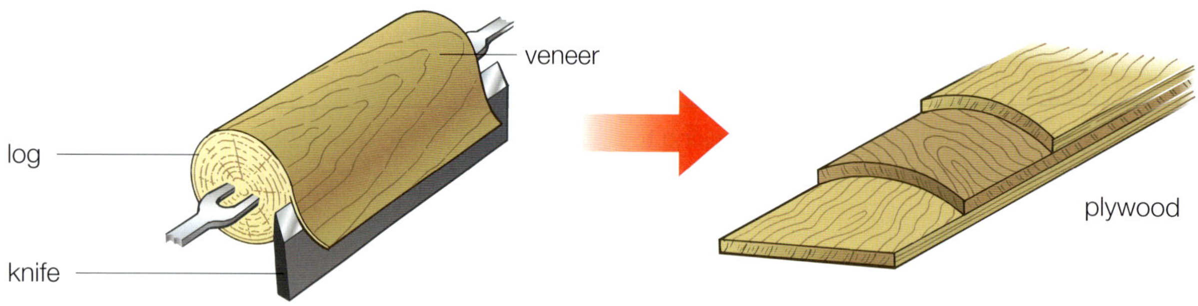

The ________[1] is fixed with two forks and turned against a ________[2]. A thin sheet of timber called a ________[3] is peeled off. It is cut to size, glued and layered to make ________[4].

2 Board types

Look at the following information about different board types and then complete the text below.

Board type	Property	Uses
plywood	flexible	boatbuilding
chipboard	easy to cut	furniture
medium density fibreboard (MDF)	easy to work	furniture

1 ________ is flexible, so it's very useful for ________.
2 ________ is used to make the carcass of cabinets because it is easy to cut.
3 Doors for cabinets are made from ____________________ because it is easy to work with.

Tip	
carcass	Korpus

3 Waste timber

What can waste timber be used for? Collect ideas with a partner and complete the diagram below.

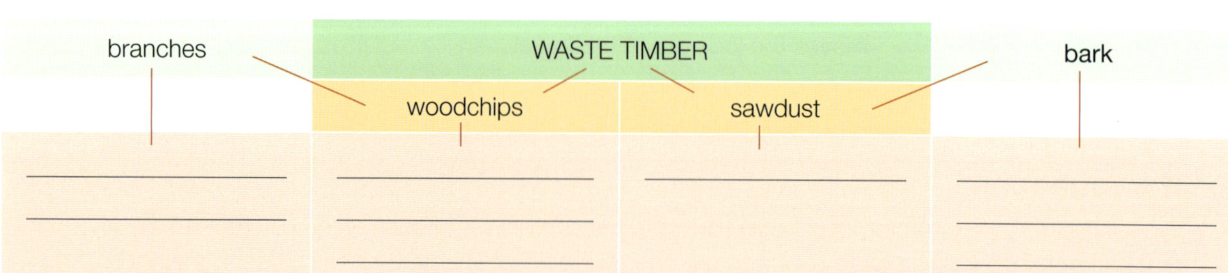

5 4 At a DIY store

A woman is in a DIY store and is asking an assistant for advice.

★ a) Listen to the recording of a customer in a DIY store asking for help and take notes. Then answer the following questions.

1 What does the customer want to make?

____

2 What material does the assistant suggest?

____

3 What does the assistant offer to do?

____

4 What does the customer give to the assistant?

____

5 What does the customer want first?

____

★★ b) Listen to the recording again and use your notes to complete this summary.

A customer in a ______________[1] asked an assistant for advice. She wanted to make a small ______________[2] but she didn't know what type of ______________[3] she should use. The assistant advised her to use ______________[4]. The customer didn't have any ______________[5], so the assistant offered to cut the wood for her. She gave him a ______________[6], but she wanted an ______________[7] first.

c) Find seven words in the word square which have something to do with timber. Use the words to write a short blog entry about manufactured boards.

Z	R	L	M	Q	H	M	I	D	G
W	N	K	N	M	U	L	C	H	H
O	W	F	R	W	B	A	R	K	N
O	L	S	K	F	X	A	H	H	A
D	O	A	V	E	N	E	E	R	T
C	G	W	G	L	L	A	T	I	U
H	L	D	R	R	W	P	S	K	A
I	I	U	P	L	Y	W	O	O	D
P	O	S	E	A	G	E	N	P	S
S	W	T	B	R	A	N	C	H	Z

1 ______________________________

2 ______________________________

3 ______________________________

4 ______________________________

5 ______________________________

6 ______________________________

7 ______________________________

IT'S YOUR TURN

Work with a partner to role-play a dialogue similar to the one in exercise 4. You can use the role cards below or your own ideas and language from the unit.

Student A

You are the customer and you want to make a bookshelf. Ask the assistant what kind of timber you should use. You also do not have all the power tools which are required. You want an estimate.

Student B

Ask the customer if you can help him/her. You advise the customer on the type of timber that should be used for a bookshelf. You ask if he/she needs any power tools. Recommend the proper power tools and make an estimate.

Extra practice: Units 1–4

1 Interview with Peter Young

Work with a partner. A local TV reporter is doing an interview with Peter Young, who owns a carpentry firm in London. Take turns to role-play the dialogue.

TV reporter	Peter Young
Begrüßen Sie Peter Young. Sagen Sie, dass Sie sich freuen, ihn kennenzulernen und fragen Sie, wie es ihm geht.	
	Bedanken Sie sich und sagen Sie, dass Sie sich ebenfalls freuen, den/die Reporter/in kennenzulernen.
Fragen Sie, welche Aufgaben ein Zimmerer/Zimmerin hat.	
	Führen Sie mindestens fünf Aufgaben eines Zimmerers / einer Zimmerin an, die Sie in den Units 1–4 gelernt haben.
Fragen Sie, welches Holz verwendet wird.	
	Zählen Sie mindestens drei verschiedene Holzarten auf.
Fragen Sie, wofür man die einzelnen Holzarten verwendet.	
	Erklären Sie, wofür man die Holzarten verwendet, die Sie aufgezählt haben.
Fragen Sie, welche Arten von Brettern verwendet werden.	
	Zählen Sie drei Arten von Brettern auf.
Bedanken Sie sich bei Peter Young für das Gespräch und verabschieden Sie sich.	
	Verabschieden Sie sich von dem/der Reporter/in.

2 Helping an American colleague

A young American apprentice is going to work at your building site for two weeks. Your boss asks you to help your colleague to find the English equivalents of the tasks listed below.

1 schwere Objekte heben und ziehen ______________________
2 Werkzeuge und Geräte bedienen ______________________
3 Werkzeuge und Geräte warten ______________________
4 Bäume fällen ______________________
5 Äste abschneiden ______________________
6 das Holz schneiden ______________________
7 die Baumstämme aus den Wald bringen ______________________
8 die Säge bedienen ______________________
9 Sperrholz produzieren ______________________
10 jemanden um Rat fragen ______________________
11 Material vorschlagen ______________________

▶▶▶ ICH KANN

		Seite / Übung
☐	Ich kann eine Rolle in einem Dialog oder einer Simulation übernehmen (z. B. in Berufssituationen). A2/9	11/4c
☐	Ich kann meine Ausbildung beziehungsweise meine gegenwärtige oder letzte berufliche Tätigkeit in einfachen Sätzen beschreiben. A2/4	5/4b
☐	Ich kann meine Meinungen, Pläne, Absichten und Ziele darlegen und einfach begründen. B1/4	5/2b
☐	Ich kann Sachverhalte (z. B. Arbeit) und Abläufe mir vertrauter Situationen (z. B. berufliche Tätigkeiten) beschreiben. B1/2	7/4b
☐	Ich kann Sachtexte verstehen, die einfach und für ein breites Publikum geschrieben sind und in denen es um Themen geht, die mit meinen Interessen oder meinem Fachgebiet in Zusammenhang stehen. B1/3	8/1
☐	Ich kann ganz einfache Arbeitsanleitungen in meiner Ausbildung oder in meinem Berufsfeld verstehen. A1/6	6/1; 8/2
☐	Ich verstehe Arbeitsanleitungen in meiner Ausbildung und am Arbeitsplatz und schriftliche Anmerkungen zu meinen eigenen Arbeiten. A2/8	6/2; 10/1, 2
☐	Ich kann kurzen und deutlich gesprochenen Texten auf Tonträgern die wesentlichen Informationen entnehmen, wenn es um vorhersehbare berufsspezifisch vertraute Dinge geht. A2/3	4/1a; 6/3; 11/4b
☐	Ich kann Interviews, Berichten und Vorträgen in den wesentlichen Punkten folgen. B1/2	9/4; 11/4a
☐	Ich kann einen kurzen, einfachen Text über ein persönliches Erlebnis oder eine Erfahrung (z. B. in der Ausbildung und im Beruf) schreiben. A2/3	5/4a, c
☐	Ich kann Listen schreiben und einfache Formulare ausfüllen. A1/5	4/1b
☐	Ich kann über meine Ausbildung und meine gegenwärtige Tätigkeit schreiben. A2/1	9/5

5 The seasoning of timber

This unit is about:	Competences:
• seasoning	• writing about seasoning
• natural seasoning	• describing seasoning in a kiln
• seasoning timber in a kiln	• listening to a recording

1 Seasoning

What do you know about the seasoning of timber? Complete the text with words from the box.

content • moisture • sap • seasoning

As a tree grows, it absorbs __________[1] through its roots.

This rises up through the roots and becomes __________[2].

When the tree is felled the moisture __________[3] is high.

The removal of this moisture is called __________[4].

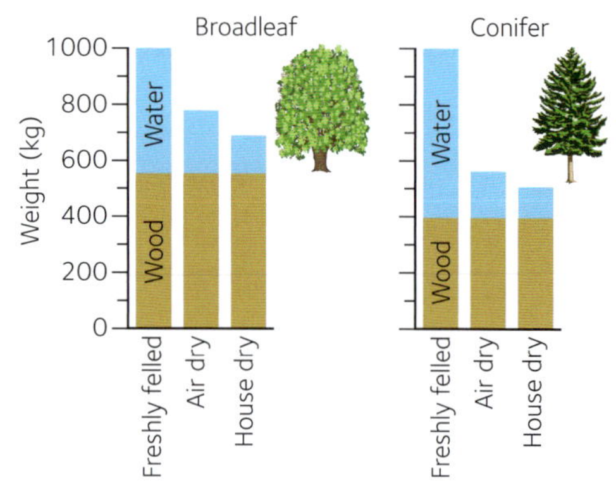

2 Natural seasoning

★ a) When you work with timber, you should know about natural seasoning. Label the illustrations with the words in orange in the text.

The freshly sawn planks are stacked in layers. Between each layer is a spacing batten. This allows air circulation around the freshly cut (green) planks. This circulation dries out the timber. This process is called stacking. The sealed ends of the planks slow down the drying-out process. This helps to prevent splitting. The stack of timber is placed under a cover. This protects the timber from both heavy rain and strong sunshine.

★★ b) Name these processes using *-ing* words.

This process is called:

1 Trees are felled for timber. __________

2 Moisture is removed from the green timber. __________

3 Planks are placed in layered stacks. __________

4 The ends of the planks are sealed. __________

★★★ c) Explain the different processes to a partner.

3 Seasoning timber in a kiln

There are different methods of seasoning timber. Work with a partner and complete the text with words from the box.

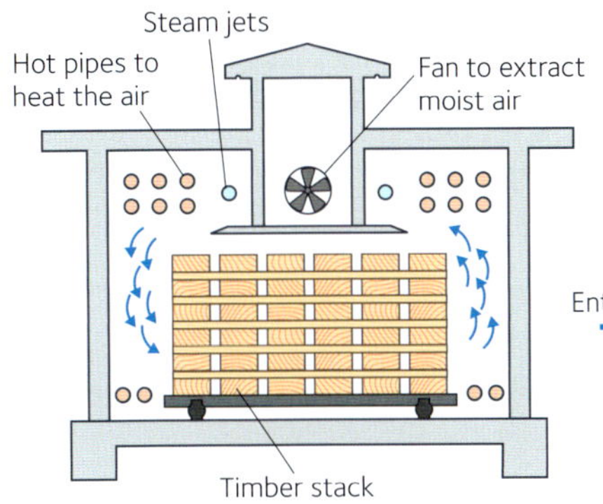

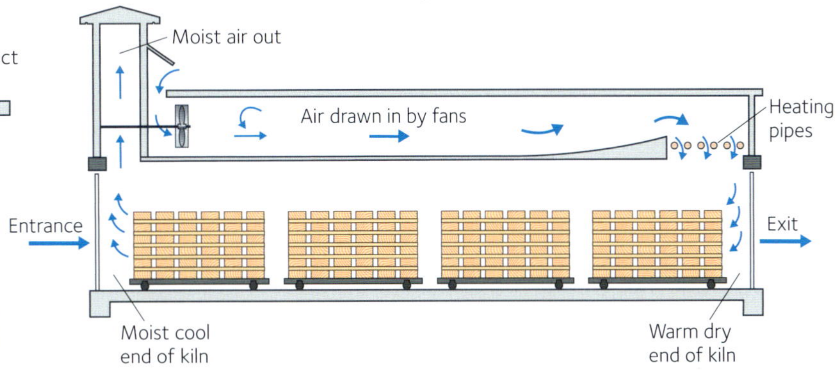

accurate • controlled • expensive • faster • high-quality • kiln • long

Seasoning timber in the traditional way is a ___________ [1] process, which can take up to a year. Today most timber is seasoned in a special drying oven called a ___________ [2]. This method is more ___________ [3] than the natural method, but this seasoning process is much more ___________ [4]. This is because the moisture content can be exactly ___________ [5] during the seasoning process. The kiln process is also ___________ [6]. This method is used to produce timber for ___________ [7] work.

6

4 The seasoned timber

The manager of a timber processing company is taking some students on a guided tour. Listen to the recording and then complete the following notes.

A There are four reasons for seasoning timber:

1 ______________________________

2 ______________________________

3 ______________________________

4 ______________________________

B The length of the seasoning process depends on three factors:

1 ______________________________

2 ______________________________

3 ______________________________

IT'S YOUR TURN

Discuss the seasoning of timber in groups of four. Answer the following questions in your discussion.

1 What does timber seasoning mean? Describe the process.

2 Why is seasoning timber important?

Sum up your discussion in a short text.

6 Defects in timber

This unit is about:
- natural defects
- seasoning defects
- insect attacks / fungus
- wood preservation

Competences:
- describing wood and its defects
- writing about insect attacks and fungus
- listening to a recording
- talking about preserving timber

1 Natural defects

If you work with wood, you should know about natural defects. Complete the text below using the words in the illustrations.

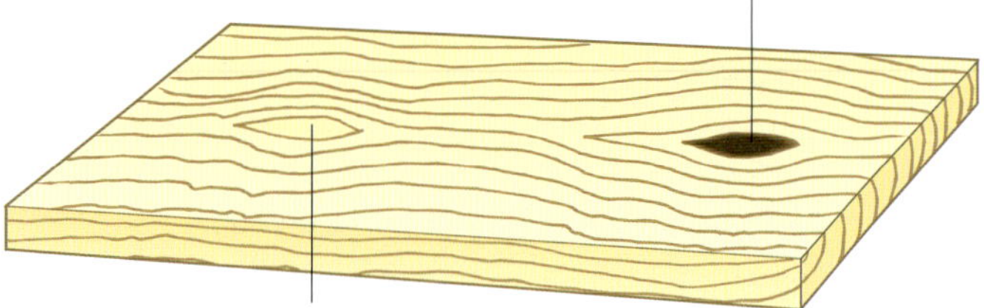

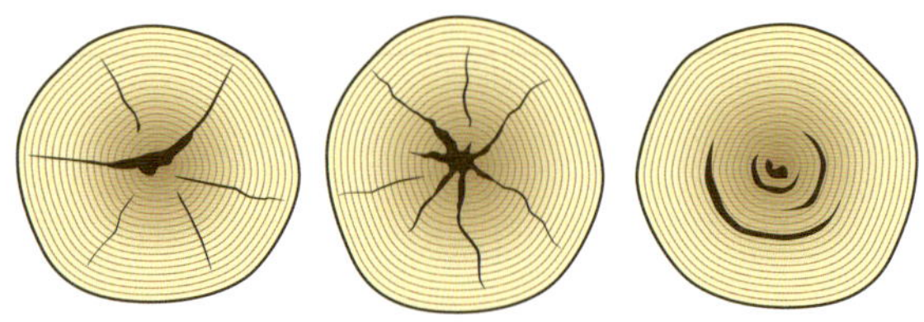

All trees grow branches and we see these in the cut timber as ____________[1]. ____________[2] spoil the wood and are serious defects. ____________[3] don't usually damage the wood and aren't a serious defect. In fact, they can give the wood "character". Pressure in the fresh timber can result in ____________[4] developing between the growth rings. Splits across the growth rings of the tree cause defects called ____________[5]. Several of these together can develop into ____________[6].

When the shake follows the growth rings it is called a ____________[7].

2 Seasoning defects

Defects can be caused by the seasoning process. Read the text and then label the pictures with the words in orange.

Trees are living organisms and contain water. As the amount of water in the timber is reduced during the seasoning process, the wood shrinks in size. Some shrinkage is normal, but if it occurs too quickly, it can cause the following defects in the timber:

Cupping – the timber bends across its width and across the grain.
Bowing – the timber bends along its length and along the grain.
Splitting – the timber splits across the grain.
Warping – the timber twists itself into a propeller shape.

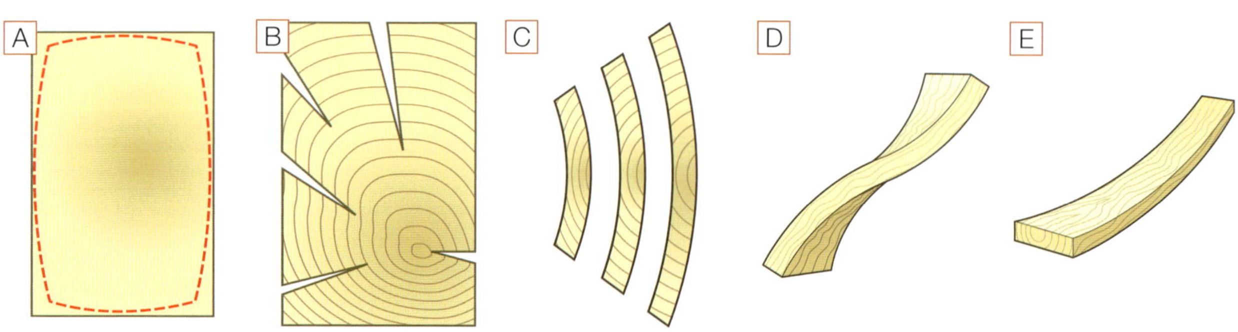

A ____________ B ____________ C ____________ D ____________ E ____________

3 Insect attack

What effects can insects have on timber? Complete the text with words from the box.

eggs • exit holes • fine powder • grubs • starch

Some insects attack wood to feed on the ________ 1. Other insects lay their ________ 2 on the surface of the wood. After they hatch, the ________ 3 bore long tunnels and chambers deep into the wood. As they feed they leave a trail of ________ 4 behind them. The mature beetles leave small ________ 5 when they leave the log.

Fotolia.com / Henrik Larsson

Tip

hatch	schlüpfen
bore	bohren

4 Fungus

Fungus can also damage wood. Complete the text with words from the box.

cellulose • moisture • spores • ventilation • weather

Fungi are a type of primitive plant. They feed on the ________ 1 in the timber. The ________ 2 of the fungi spread quickly and the wood rots. Seasoning reduces the ________ 3 content of timber to below 18%, which helps to prevent rot. Good ________ 4 also helps to preserve the timber. Timber which is exposed to the ________ 5 should always be treated with a preservative.

7

5 Wood preservation

A man wants to build a fence and needs some information about preserving timber so he asks an assistant at a DIY store for advice.

★ a) Listen to the recording and take notes. Then complete the sentences.

1 Preserving timber prevents decay caused by ________ .
2 This process can also protect the timber against attack by ________ .
3 With ready treated wood, the preservative is applied under ________ .
4 Ready-treated wood gives longer-lasting ________ .
5 Wood preservative is usually toxic, so the person applying it must wear protective clothing, gloves and a ________ .

Tip

You should …
You'd better …
Remember to …

★★ b) What do you do at your company to preserve timber? Collect ideas in a group and take notes. What are the three most common techniques used to preserve timber?

★★★ c) Make up a dialogue in a DIY store and act it out in front of your class. Use the phrases from the recording from exercise 5a.

Customer	Assistant
You want to make a garden gate made of timber. You want to last it for as long as possible.	You give the customer some advice about treating timber with a preservative and about ready-treated wood.

IT'S YOUR TURN

Work with a partner to make a list of possible defects in timber. Go on the Internet and find pictures to illustrate these defects. Present these pictures in class.

7 Drawing and sketching (Part 1)

This unit is about:
- equipment for sketching
- skills for sketching
- drawing

Competences:
- describing sketching equipment
- talking about pencil grades
- writing about sketching skills
- listening to a recording

1 Basic equipment for sketching

Freehand sketches give you an idea of what a piece of furniture should look like.

★ a) Read the text below and then label the photos with words from the text.

Making freehand sketches of something you want to make is a very useful step before producing an exact technical drawing – and much faster. You need very little equipment for sketching – three or four pencils of various grades. Your pencils must be sharp, so you'll need a pencil sharpener and an eraser for removing errors.

1

____

2

____

3

____

4

____

★★ b) Talk about the different grades of pencil with a partner. The useful words and phrases will help you.

The letter … means the pencil is …
The number … means the pencil is …
Grade … is best for …
Grade … is more suitable for …

Tip		
hard	harder	(the) hardest
soft	softer	(the) softest
accurate	more accurate	(the) most accurate

8

2 Sketching skills

For an experienced craftsperson, a good working sketch is usually enough. If a technical drawing is necessary, it is usually produced by an architect or a structural engineer.

★ a) Label the drawings with the terms in orange.

Using a grid: This helps you to draw complex details and to show their relative sizes as accurately as possible without producing a technical drawing.
Dimensioning: Sizes (length, width, depth, height) are now added to the working drawing.
Rendering: You can indicate round and curved shapes by using shading or crosshatching. This also makes a sketch look solid and more realistic.

1
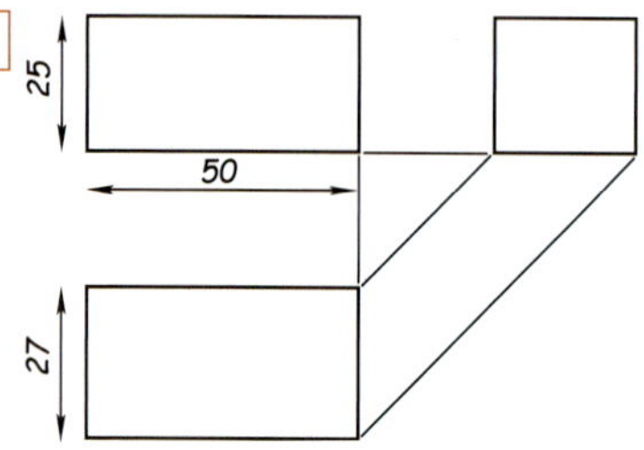

____

2
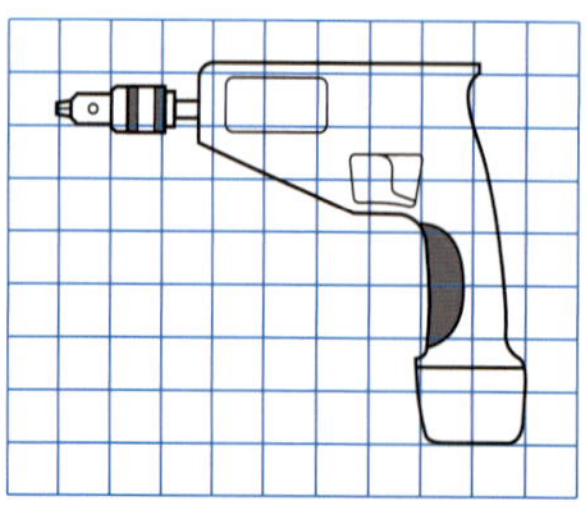
____

3
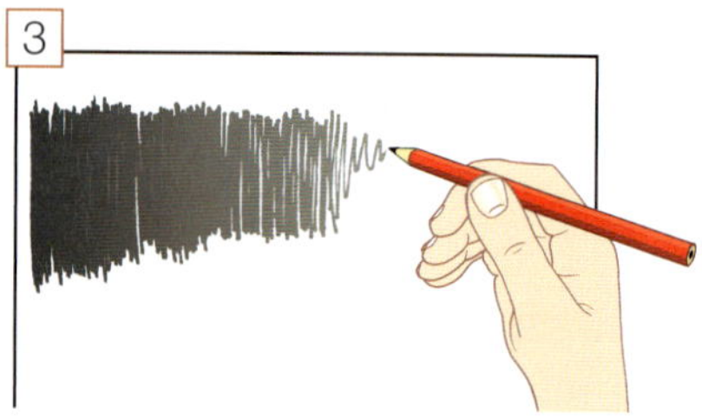
____

★★ b) Listen to the recording of a carpenter telling his apprentice about sketching and then complete the text with words from the box.

artist • curved • freehand • grades • horizontal • inclined • line • ruler • sketch • skills • soft • thin • vertical

To make a sketch you'll need a few simple drawing ________[1], but you don't need to be an ________[2]! Producing a working ________[3] is a ________[4] activity, so you don't even need a ________[5]. Some lines are ________[6] or ________[7]. Other lines are ________[8] or ________[9]. Most people use a pencil for sketching and there are different ________[10] of pencil for the different types of ________[11] you might need for your sketch. These range from pencils that will give you broad, ________[12] lines with lots of contrast, to pencils that produce very exact, ________[13] lines with very little contrast.

9

3 Drawing

★ a) Listen to the recording of a new student asking her teacher for some help with her drawing project and take notes.

Notes

____

____

____

____

★★ b) Work with a partner to answer the questions below. Use your notes from exercise 1a.

1 What does the student want to make?

____

2 Why does she need help?

____

3 What does the teacher give her?

____

4 Why does he give her this?

____

5 What does she draw first?

____

6 How are they labelled?

____

Listen again to check your answers.

IT'S YOUR TURN

Work with a partner to make a mind map with useful information from this unit.

8 Drawing and sketching (Part 2)

This unit is about:	Competences:
• sketching and drawing • drawing on the computer • numbers	• describing sketches and construction drawings • listening to a dialogue about computer drawings

1 Sketching and drawing

Carpenters should know how to sketch a construction drawing. Write two sentences using the sentence parts below.

A technical drawing	is a rough draft of	and detailed design.
A sketch	is an exact	what your piece of furniture will look like.

2 Drafting tools and drafting table

Computer-aided drafting is common practice today, but sometimes it is still useful to produce pencil graphics on a drawing board or drafting table.

★ a) Label the different tools with words from the box.

1

Shutterstock / SmileStudio

2

Shutterstock / Alexander Zaun

3
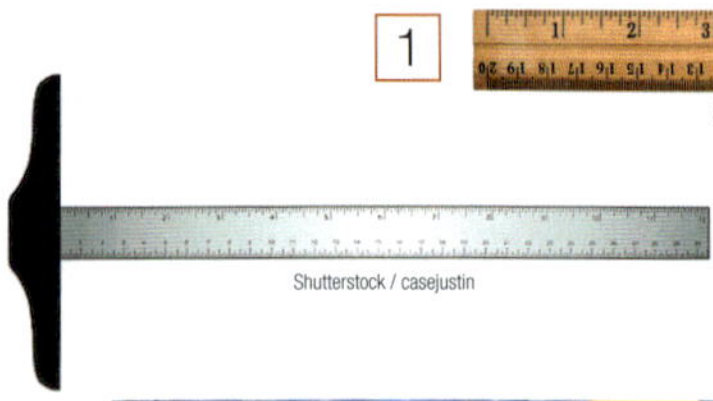
Shutterstock / casejustin

4

Shutterstock / RGtimeline

5
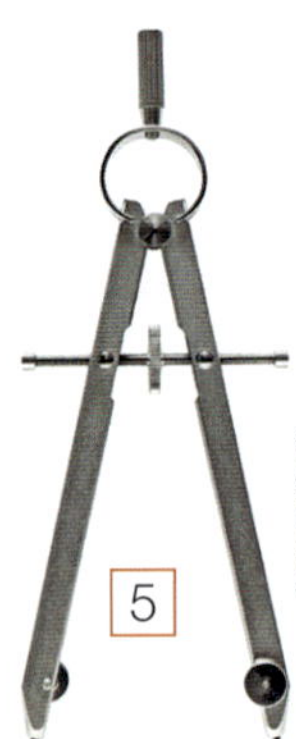
Shutterstock / Gena96

6

Shutterstock / Vik Y

Technical drawing tools:
pen and pencil
drawing board
T-square
French curves
ruler
compass

★★ b) Explain how to build a drafting table.
The illustration and the phrases will help you.

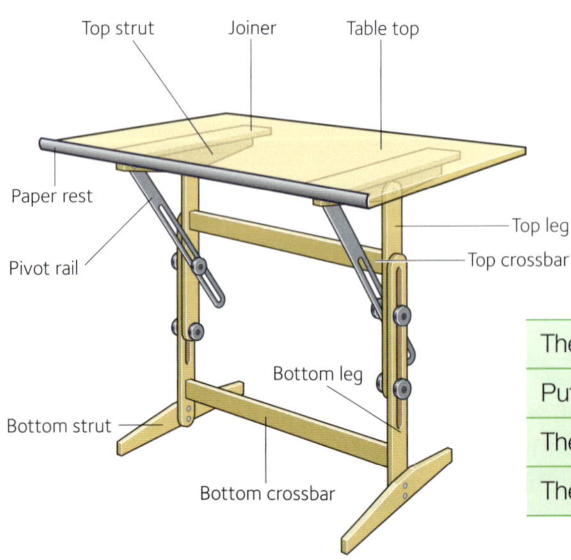

Tip	
table top	Tischplatte
top strut	obere Stütze
paper rest	Papierablage
pivot rail	Drehschiene
top leg	oberes Bein
top crossbar	oberer Querbalken

The bottom crossbar / … is connected to the bottom strut / …
Put the bottom leg / … on top of the strut /…
The pivotal rail connects the … with the …
The table top / … is on top of / below the …

3 How to draw a chair

Here is a mixed-up description of how to draw a chair. Put the sentences in the correct order.

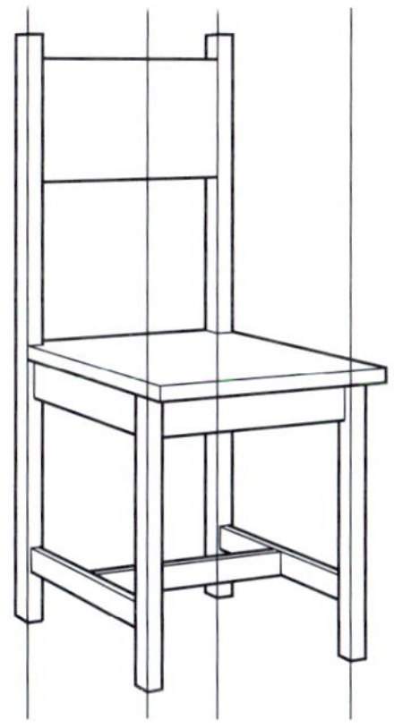

___ Draw a horizontal line connecting all four vertical lines in the middle. This will look like a parallelogram.

___ Add volume to the outline you have made.

___ Draw a square on top of the parallelogram.
Darken the vertical lines below the parallelogram.
These will be the chair's legs.

___ Draw four vertical lines.

10

4 Drawing on the computer

★ a) Peter Young is giving apprentice Patti White some advice about drawing on the computer. Listen to the dialogue and then complete the text below.

download • program • course • computer-aided design • software • animation

Patti White: Excuse me, Mr Young. I've got a question about drawing on the computer.

Peter Young: Sure, Patti. How can I help you?

Patti: What kinds of ________________[1] can I use to draw a plan?

Peter: The carpenters at Young Enterprises use different kinds of CAD software.

Patti: CAD? What does CAD mean?

Peter: CAD means ______________________[2].
Programs that are used for drawing and sketching are called CAD programs.

Patti: I see. I've heard the term before, but I didn't know what it means.

Peter: There are many different programs on the market. If you want to try what it is like to draw on the computer, you can ____________________[3] a free ______________[4].

Patti: That's a good idea! Does it take long to learn how to use a CAD program?

Peter: Some programs are easy to use, especially programs that are used for sketching.
Other programs are more complicated, because they have many functions, such as 3D ____________________[5].

Patti: That sounds really interesting. How can I get to know one of these programs?

Peter: Well, one of our experienced carpenters can show you the basics. But I would suggest that you attend a ________________[6] on CAD software. I can register you for one if you'd like.

Patti: That would be great! Thank you!

Listen again and check your answers.

★★ b) Discuss the following questions in groups. What software do you use in your company? How do you draw sketches? Collect the pros and cons of the different programs.

IT'S YOUR TURN

Go on the Internet with a partner and look for free design software. Try it and draw a simple plan with it. Present your results in class.

Extra practice: Units 5–8

1 Blog entry about carpentry

A new magazine has published a series of articles about your trade. You are asked to write a blog entry for the magazine's online edition. Your topic is "construction drawings in carpentry".

Answer the following questions in your blog entry.

1 Why are sketches and construction drawings important?
2 Who draws them in your company?
3 Is it easy for you to sketch/draw?
4 What are the differences between drawings made by hand and computer-aided drawings? Which do you prefer and why?

2 PowerPoint presentation

Work in groups of three. Find appropriate pictures, facts and figures about seasoning timber on the Internet and then make a PowerPoint presentation.

Include the following aspects:

1 What does seasoning timber mean?
2 How does seasoning timber work?
3 Why is seasoning timber important?
4 What natural defects of timber are there?
5 What are the consequences of these defects?
6 What can you do to help prevent these defects occurring?

Shutterstock / Syda Productions

Now carry out the presentation in class.

▶▶▶ ICH KANN

	Seite/Übung
☐ Ich kann ein Gespräch über mir vertraute Themen beginnen, in Gang halten und beenden. B1/1	17/5b; 18/1b
☐ Ich kann eine Rolle in einem Dialog oder einer Simulation übernehmen (z. B. Berufssituation). A2/9	17/5c
☐ Ich kann Sachverhalte (z. B. Arbeit) und Abläufe mir vertrauter Situationen (z. B. berufliche Tätigkeiten) beschreiben. B1/2	15/2c; 21/4b
☐ Ich kann mit Hilfe vorgegebener Wörter oder Illustrationen einfache Geschichten und Beschreibungen von Abläufen vorbereiten und erzählen. A2/6	15/ It's your turn
☐ Ich kann Sachtexte verstehen, die einfach und für ein breites Publikum geschrieben sind und in denen es um Themen geht, die mit meinen Interessen oder meinem Fachgebiet in Zusammenhang stehen. B1/3	14/1, 2a; 16/1; 17/3, 4
☐ Ich kann Informationen in verschiedenen längeren Texten oder Textteilen finden, die ich brauche, um eine bestimmte Aufgabe zu lösen. B1/8	16/2; 18/1a
☐ Ich kann ganz einfache Arbeitsanleitungen in meiner Ausbildung oder in meinem Berufsfeld verstehen. A1/6	18/2a; 21/3
☐ Ich kann kurzen und deutlich gesprochenen Texten auf Tonträgern die wesentlichen Informationen entnehmen, wenn es um vorhersehbare alltägliche oder berufsspezifisch vertraute Dinge geht. A2/3	17/5a; 19/2b
☐ Ich kann Arbeitsabläufen im Wesentlichen folgen (z. B. Sicherheitsanweisungen, Bedienungsanleitungen). A2/7	15/4
☐ Ich kann Interviews, Berichten und Vorträgen in den wesentlichen Punkten folgen. B1/2	19/3a, b; 21/4a
☐ Ich kann einen kurzen, einfachen Text über ein persönliches Erlebnis oder eine Erfahrung (z. B. in der Ausbildung und im Beruf) schreiben. A2/3	17/ It's your turn

9 Hand tools (Part 1)

This unit is about:
- tools
- saws and chisels

stecheisen

Competences:
- writing about tools
- talking about tools
- describing tools and their use

1 Tools for measuring and marking

★ a) Read the text and then label the illustrations of the tools with the words in orange.

If you want to cut a piece of timber to a certain length, first measure the length you want with a tape measure and then mark it with a soft pencil. To cut the timber accurately, this mark should be extended into a straight line. A thick piece of timber might need to be cut from several sides, and in such cases, the line you have made on one side must be continued around the other three sides of the timber. This is called "squaring" and to do this you will need a try square. If you want to mark an inclined line, you should use an adjustable bevel. You can adjust this to the angle you want or hold it against an object which has an inclined plane. You can now transfer this angle onto the timber.

1

Shutterstock / Joe Belanger

adjustable bevel

2

Shutterstock / stanalex

try square

3

Shutterstock / Seregam

tape measure

dick is 10cm long

★★ b) The three tools below are all used for marking out measurements on timber, but what they mark out is different. Do you know the German names for these tools?

1 marking gauge ~~sehr~~ streichmaß

2 mortise gauge doppeltes streichmaß

3 trammel Zirkel

★★★ c) Work with a partner. What do you use the tools for? Have you used any of the tools before?

Tip

• transfer angles for very fine, accurate work	• Winkel für sehr feine und genaue Arbeiten übertragen
• draw parallel lines	• parallele Linien zeichnen
• measure widths	• die Breite abmessen
• mark curves and ellipses	• Kurven und Ellipsen markieren
• draw/mark circles	• Kreise zeichnen/markieren

I've never used a … before.	I've used a … before.
What's it used for?	It's used to mark out …

2 Saws and chisels

★ a) Read the names of the tools and their uses and then label the tools below with both their English and German names.

Tip	
Tools	**Uses**
keyhole saw ✓	cutting holes, curves, complex shapes
mitre-box saw ✓	making frames, cutting exact angles
adjustable metal-cutting saw ✓	cutting metal sheets, nails, metal rods
handsaw ✓	cutting logs, branches
bowsaw ✓	sawing pieces of timber
firmer chisel Stechbeitel	cutting a trench or a slot in wood
mortise chisel	making joints, cutting a groove
carving chisel Holzschnittbeitel	freehand carving, designs
turning chisel	cutting elaborate shapes using a lathe

1
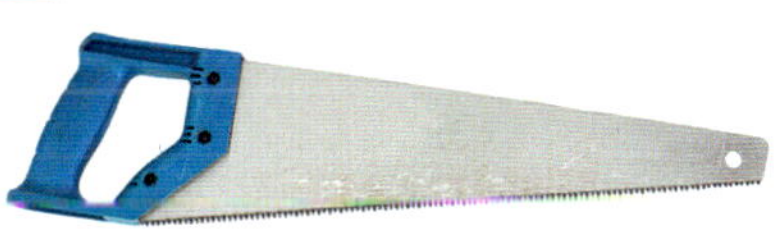
Hand saw

2
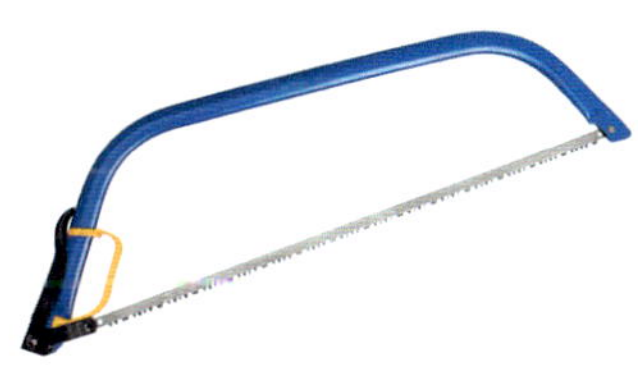
Bow saw

3

~~Hand saw~~ keyholesaw

4
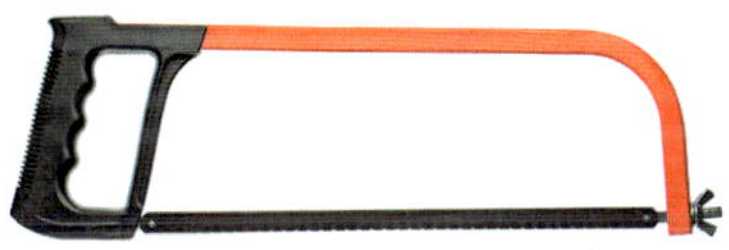
adjustable metal-cutting saw

5

Firmer chisel

6

carving chisel

7

~~mit~~ mitre-box saw

8

mortise chisel

9

turning chisel

★★ b) Work with a partner to discuss which tool is best for the job.

I want to …	You'll need a … for that.

IT'S YOUR TURN

Work with a partner. Choose three of the tools from unit 9 and write down exact descriptions of how to use these tools. Present the results in class.

10 Hand tools (Part 2)

This unit is about:
- parts of a chisel
- a carpenter's ratchet brace
- boring holes

Competences:
- describing tools
- writing about a carpenter's ratchet brace
- listening to a recording

1 Tools

★ a) Label the tools below with their English names and then do the crossword puzzle.

axe • C-clamp • hammer • hatchet • mallet • mitre • pincers • plane • rasp • spirit level

1
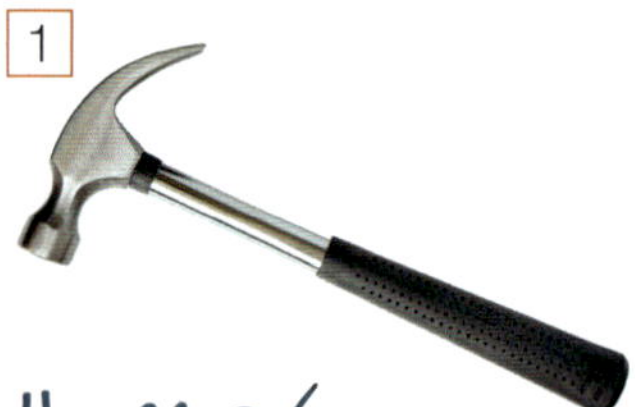
Hammer
Shutterstock / revers

2

MAlleT
Shutterstock / Li Chaoshu

3
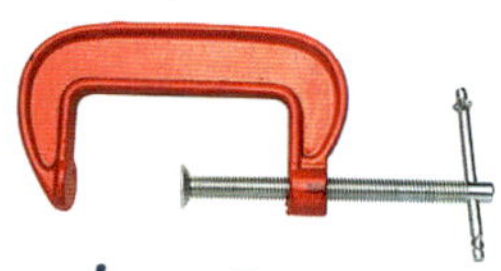
c-clamp
Shutterstock / ownway

4

spirit level
Shutterstock / Iakov Filimonov

5
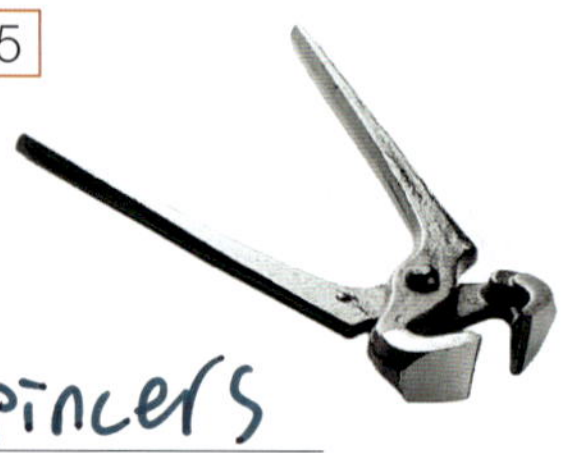
Pincers
Shutterstock / humbak

6

Rasp
Shutterstock / agolndr

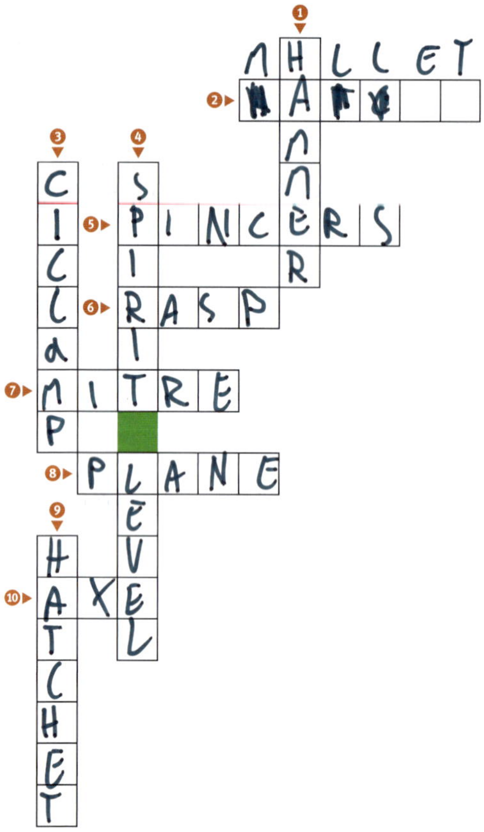

7

Mitre
Shutterstock / sauletas

8

Plane
Shutterstock / mikeledray

9

Hatchet
Shutterstock / Jaroslaw Soltysiak

10
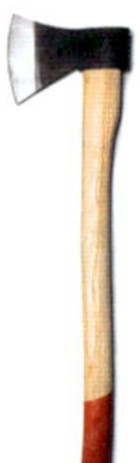
Axe
Shutterstock / Ehur

★★ b) Work with a partner. What are the different tools from exercise 1a used for?

chopping wood • hitting nails/pegs • holding two parts together • making wood smooth / making rough timber smooth • pulling out nails • testing if a surface is level • sawing angles

e.g. Pincers are used for ... / A mitre is used for ...

2 Parts of a chisel

A chisel consists of several parts. Read the text and then label the illustration with the words in orange.

The blade of the chisel is shaped at one end so that it has a ground edge and a cutting edge. The other end forms a sharp spike. This is called a tang and it fits into the wooden handle. A shoulder prevents the tang from being pushed up into the handle and thus splitting the timber. A steel ferrule is also used to prevent the timber splitting.

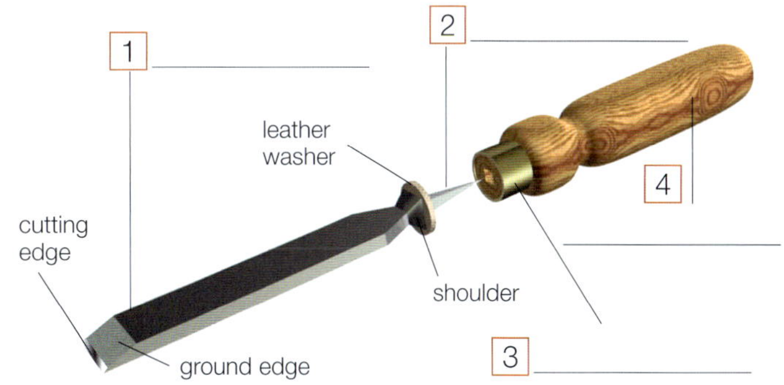

3 A carpenter's ratchet brace

What are the parts of a ratchet brace for? Look at the drawing and then complete the sentences.

1 The ______________ is the diameter of the turn of the brace.
2 The ______________ allows the handle to move smoothly.
3 The ______________ closes on the bit and holds it in position.
4 The ______________ changes the handle's direction of movement.
5 The ______________ controls the direction of the turn.

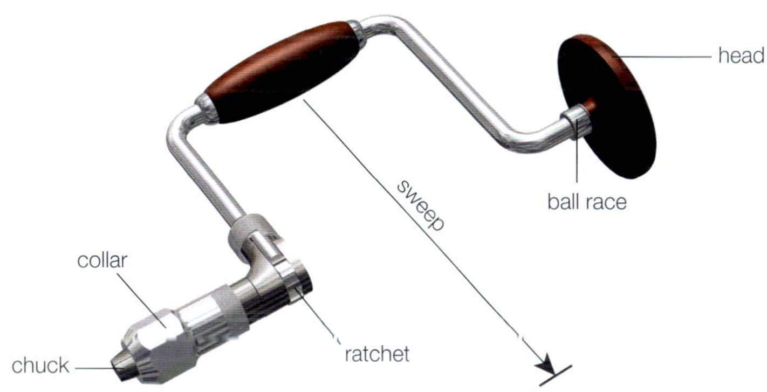

11 ## 4 Boring holes

Maria, a student, wants to bore a hole in a piece of pine. She asks Mr Price, her teacher, for advice. Listen to the recording and take notes. Then complete the answers.

1 How wide should the first hole be? It should be ______________ millimetres wide.
2 How deep should the hole be? ______________
3 What stops the bit at the correct depth? ______________
4 How wide should the second hole be? ______________
5 What should Maria use for this hole? ______________

IT'S YOUR TURN

Work with a partner to answer the following questions about the tools from the unit.
What are the tools used for? Which tools have you used before? Which ones haven't you used?
Write a short text about your experiences with the different tools.

11 Portable power tools

This unit is about:
- basic power tools
- a DIY store

Competences:
- describing power tools
- listening to a dialogue at a DIY store
- acting out a dialogue

1 Basic power tools

★ a) Label the power tools below with words from the box.

belt sander • circular saw • drill • glue gun • jigsaw • nail gun • orbital sander • portable planer • reciprocating saw • router

1

Shutterstock / Dinga
____

2
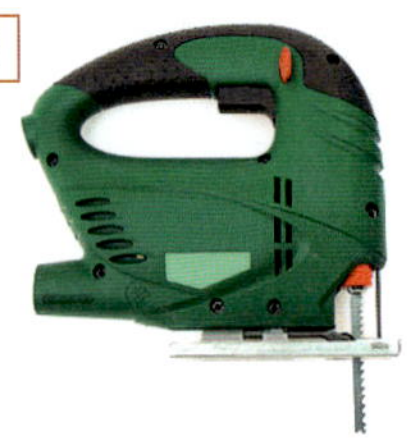
Shutterstock / Igor Kolos
____

3
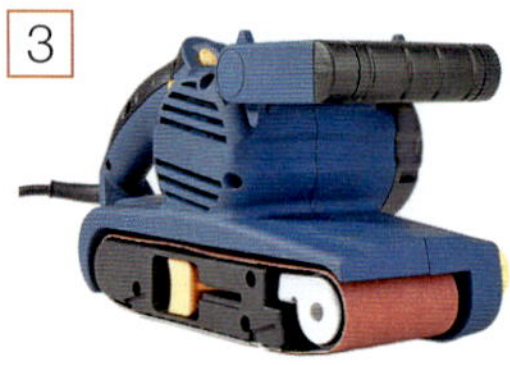
Shutterstock / Norman Pogson
____

4

Shutterstock / Photoexpert
____

5

Shutterstock / Mayovskyy Andrew
____

6
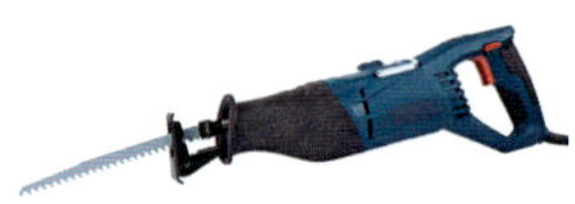
Shutterstock / Eugen Shatilo
____

7

Shutterstock / MNI
____

8

Shutterstock / Miguel Garcia Saavedra
____

9

Shutterstock / Nils Z
____

10

Shutterstock / Photoexpert
____

★★ b) Complete these descriptions with the names of the tools above.

1 The ______________________ is used to bore holes.
2 The ______________________ is used to mould the timber.
3 The ______________________ is used to do heavy sanding.
4 The ______________________ is used to cut curves.
5 The ______________________ is used to cut planks and heavy timber.
6 The ______________________ is used to cut sheet material into strips.
7 The ______________________ is used to do light sanding.
8 The ______________________ is used to melt and apply glue.
9 The ______________________ is used to drive nails into wood or other materials.
10 The ______________________ is used to reduce the thickness of timber.

12

2 In a DIY store

Mr Clarke is in a DIY store. He wants to buy an electric drill, but he isn't sure what model he should buy. The assistant there is a qualified carpenter and can give him some expert advice.

★ a) Listen to the recording and take notes in your textbook.

____

____

★★ b) Use your notes to answer the questions below. Listen to the dialogue again and check your answers.

1 What does Mr Clarke want to buy? ______________________

2 Which three types of drill does the assistant mention?

____

3 What does Mr Clarke need the drill for?

____

4 Why is the first drill unsuitable?

____

5 Why is the second drill more suitable?

____

____

6 Which other things can the drill be used for?

____

7 What extras come with the drill? ______________________

IT'S YOUR TURN

Role-play a dialogue in a DIY store with a partner. One of you is the customer, the other one is an assistant in a DIY store. The phrases in the boxes will help you.

Assistant in DIY store	Customer in DIY store
Good morning/afternoon.	Good morning/afternoon.
Can I help you? / Do you need some advice?	I need … / I'm looking for …
We have a wide range of drills/sanders/… over here.	I want to use it for …
This model is for amateurs/professionals.	It's too expensive/small/…
What do you want to use it for?	It isn't big/powerful/… enough.
Where do you want to use it?	How fast/heavy/powerful/… is it?
This model comes with a … metre cable.	Can I use it outside?
With this model, you get these extras: …	What extras does it come with?
The price is very reasonable.	How long does the guarantee last?
It's only … pounds/euros/dollars/…	How much is it?

12 Machinery in the workshop

This unit is about:	Competences:
• machines in the workshop	• listening to a recording
• using a bench saw	• writing about a bench saw
• safety	• describing machines in the workshop

13 🎧 **1**

Machines in the workshop

★ a) Listen to the recording of a carpenter showing some students around a workshop and then label the machine tools below with words from the box.

mortiser • band saw • lathe • planer • bench saw

1

Shutterstock / Dmitry Kalinovsky

____

2

Shutterstock / Maksim Dubinsky

____

3

Shutterstock / m.bonotto

____

4

Shutterstock / B Brown

____

5

Shutterstock / m.bonotto

____

★★ b) Listen to the recording again. Which machines should you use for the jobs below?

Timber for a carport

1 Smooth out the lengths of rough timber. ______________________

2 Cut the timber into lengths. ______________________

3 Produce the round posts. ______________________

4 Produce the curved pieces of timber. ______________________

5 Cut out mortises in the round post and curved pieces. ______________________

2 Using a bench saw

As a carpenter, you should know how to use a bench saw. Read the text below and then use the words in orange to label the illustration.

There are two control wheels. These move the cast-iron saw table in various directions.
The switch box is always at the front of the machine. The green button on the left is START.
The red button on the right is STOP.
The sawblade is partly covered by a blade guard. You must hold the timber firmly against the fence during the cutting process. The fence can be moved and secured by a locking lever.

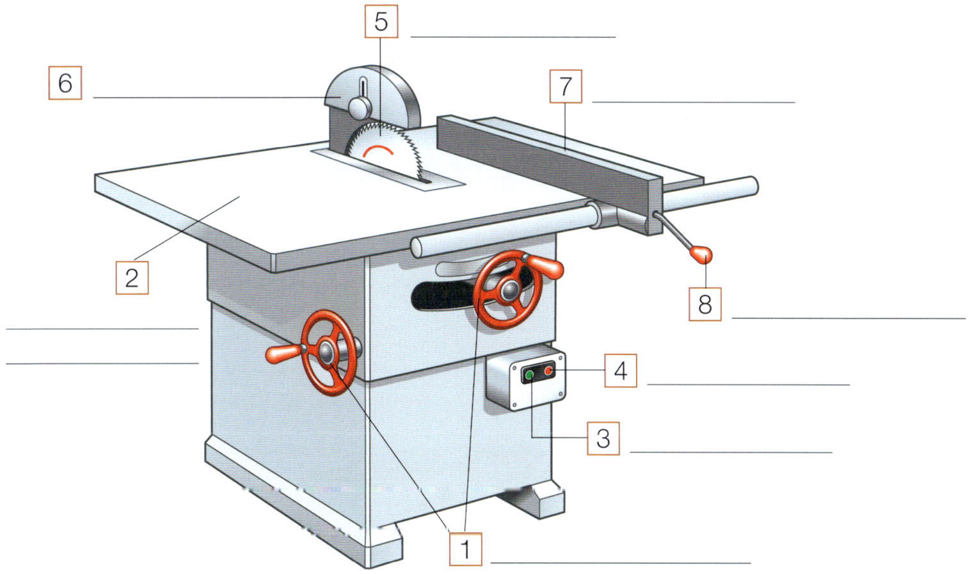

14

3 A safety talk

Listen to the recording of a safety officer explaining safety measures to some new apprentices and take notes. Then answer the questions.

1 Where is the safety officer meeting the new apprentices?

2 Where is the main switch?

3 Why is it so important?

4 When should the apprentices use this switch?

5 What are the two buttons on each machine for?

6 How is the air in the workshop cleaned?

7 What's the most important thing to know about any machine?

IT'S YOUR TURN

Class discussion. Talk about the use of the machines in exercises 1 and 2.

1 What is each of the machines used for? Which machines have/haven't you used before? What safety measures are important when you use one of these machines?
2 Write down a short summary of the discussion.

Extra practice: Units 9–12

1 Vocabulary quiz

★ a) Label the tools with words from the boxes.

carpenter's rule • C-clamp • jigsaw • wood • spirit level • belt sander • nail gun

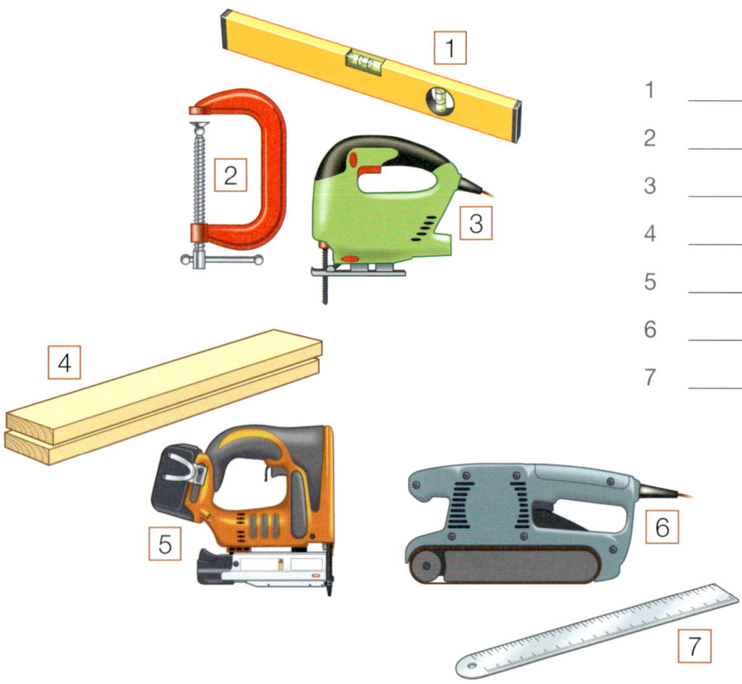

1 ______________________
2 ______________________
3 ______________________
4 ______________________
5 ______________________
6 ______________________
7 ______________________

hammer • hatchet • hand saw • brace • plane • chisel • mitre • mallet • try square • rasp • tape measure • pincers

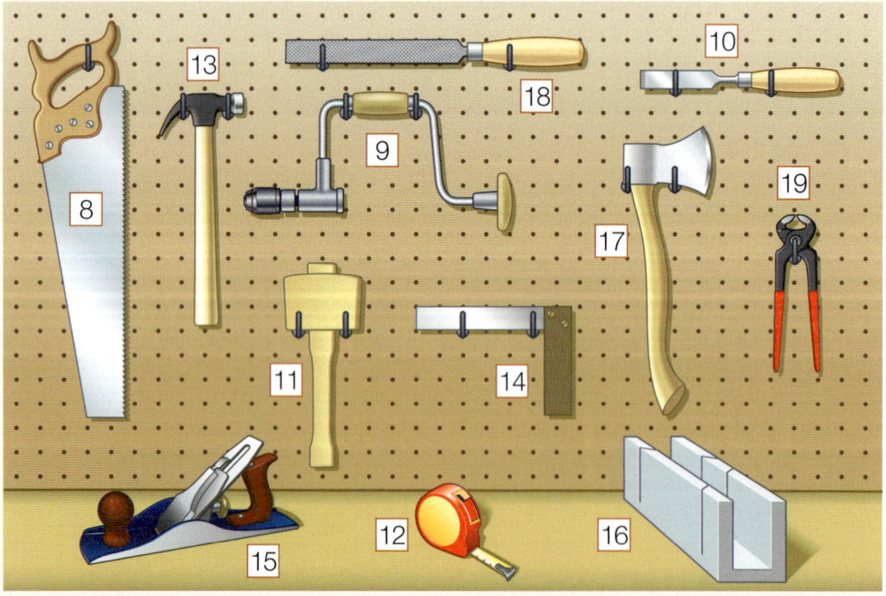

8 ______________________
9 ______________________
10 ______________________
11 ______________________
12 ______________________
13 ______________________
14 ______________________
15 ______________________
16 ______________________
17 ______________________
18 ______________________
19 ______________________

★★ b) Work with a partner to describe what the tools above are used for.

2 Group project

There is an open day at your school and your teacher asks you to present some information about tools and machinery in the workshop. Get together in groups of three and make a poster presentation about the most important aspects from units 9 to 12.

Summarize the essential information about:
- hand tools
- portable power tools
- machinery in the workshop

Find pictures, interesting facts and statistics on the Internet. Present your poster in class.

▶▶▶ ICH KANN

	Seite / Übung
☐ Ich kann ein Gespräch über mir vertraute Themen beginnen, in Gang halten und beenden. B1/1	24/1c; 25/2b
☐ Ich kann eine Rolle in einem Dialog oder einer Simulation übernehmen (z. B. Berufssituation). A2/9	29/ It's your turn
☐ Ich kann Sachverhalte (z. B. Arbeit) und Abläufe mir vertrauter Situationen (z. B. berufliche Tätigkeiten) beschreiben. B1/2	27/ It's your turn
☐ Ich kann Sachtexte verstehen, die einfach und für ein breites Publikum geschrieben sind und in denen es um Themen geht, die mit meinen Interessen oder meinem Fachgebiet in Zusammenhang stehen. B1/3	27/3
☐ Ich kann Informationen in verschiedenen längeren Texten oder Textteilen finden, die ich brauche, um eine bestimmte Aufgabe zu lösen. B1/8	24/1a; 27/2; 31/2
☐ Ich kann ganz einfache Arbeitsanleitungen in meiner Ausbildung oder in meinem Berufsfeld verstehen. A1/6	28/1b
☐ Ich kann kurzen und deutlich gesprochenen Texten auf Tonträgern die wesentlichen Informationen entnehmen, wenn es um vorhersehbare alltägliche oder berufsspezifisch vertraute Dinge geht. A2/3	29/2a, b; 30/1a, b
☐ Ich kann einfachen Beschreibungen von Vorgängen und Arbeitsabläufen im Wesentlichen folgen (z. B. Sicherheitsanweisungen). A2/7	31/3
☐ Ich kann Interviews, Berichten und Vorträgen in den wesentlichen Punkten folgen. B1/2	27/4
☐ Ich kann einfache beschreibende Texte zu grundlegenden Sachverhalten oder Aufgabenstellungen aus meinem Fachbereich (z. B. Technik) verfassen. B1/4	25/ It's your turn
☐ Ich kann einen kurzen, einfachen Text über ein persönliches Erlebnis oder eine Erfahrung (z. B. in der Ausbildung und im Beruf) schreiben. A2/3	24/1b

13 Health and safety

This unit is about:
- safety rules in the workshop
- safety rules on the building site
- protection

Competences:
- writing about safety rules
- describing protection
- listening to a recording

1 Safety rules in the workshop

In the workshop, you should follow certain safety rules. Complete the text using words from the box.

contact • cut off • escape • safety officer

If I work with machines, …

1 I should know who the _______________ is and where he or she is.
2 I need to know how to _______________ that person in an emergency.
3 I must also know the quickest _______________ route out of the workshop.
4 I must know how to _______________ the power supply safely.

2 Safety rules on the building site

Before you can start work on a building site, you have to know some safety rules. Complete the text below using words from the box.

first-aid • know • overhead • work area

A building site can be a very dangerous place, so I must always keep my personal _______________ [1] clean and tidy. I must know where the _______________ [2] station is. I must check for _______________ [3] power lines. And, above all, I must _______________ [4] the safety rules and respect them.

3 Protection

★ a) Protection is very important on a building site. Read the text and then label the illustrations with words from the text.

I am expected to wear ear protectors to prevent hearing damage. I wear safety goggles to protect my eyes from being damaged by pieces of timber or metal. My mouth is covered by a respirator mask so that dust can't get into my lungs. My feet are protected by safety boots with steel toe caps and protective gloves cover my hands. My head is protected from falling objects by a safety helmet.

A
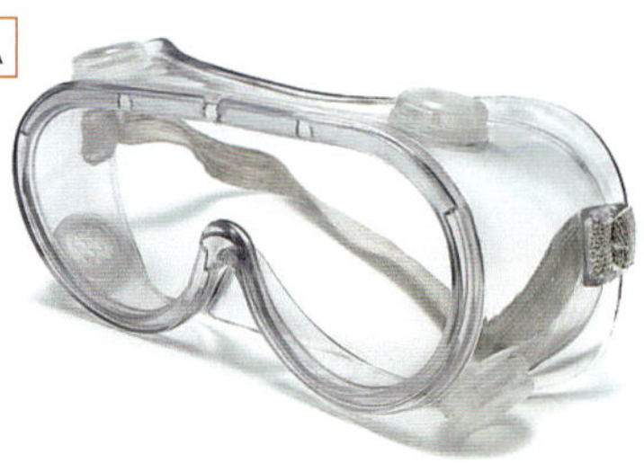

____

B

____

C

____

D

Shutterstock / Everything

E

Shutterstock / Anke van Wyk

F
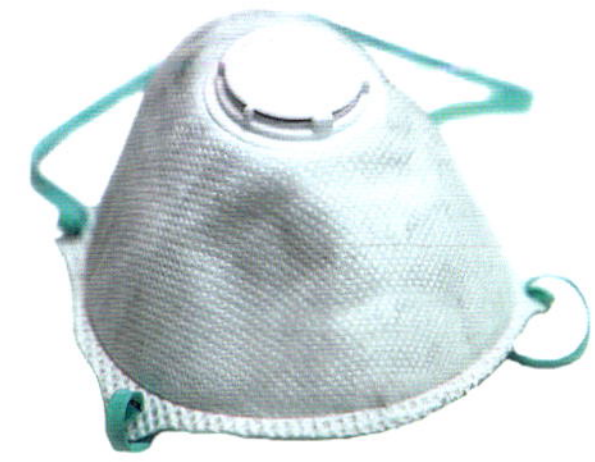
Shutterstock / Aleksandar Mijatovic

★★ b) Write the meaning of the sign and its purpose under each picture.

1 ____________

2 ____________

3 ____________

4 ____________

5 ____________

6 ____________

	Meaning		Purpose
A	No smoking!	a	to prevent your clothes getting caught in a machine
B	Beware of faulty power cables!	b	to prevent electrocution
C	Wear safety goggles!	c	to prevent foot injury
D	No loose clothing!	d	to prevent fire
E	Keep your workspace clear!	e	to prevent tripping/falling
F	Wear safety boots!	f	to prevent eye injury

15

4 A site safety talk

Mr Blunder, the site safety officer, is explaining the basic safety procedures to an apprentice. Listen to the recording and take notes. Then answer the questions.

1 What is the talk about? ____________

2 What does the apprentice want to know first? ____________

3 Where's the first aid station? ____________

4 What's near the first-aid station? ____________

5 What is on the sign on the first-aid station? ____________

6 What is the first thing to do after an accident? ____________

7 If you see an accident, what should you do?

____

8 Why shouldn't you move an injured person?

____

9 What can you do for the injured person?

____

10 What should you do after the accident? ____________

IT'S YOUR TURN

Write down the five safety rules you have found most useful in this unit. Who is the safety officer at your company? What safety rules do you have on the building site?

14 Nails and fasteners

This unit is about:
- parts of a nail
- types of nail
- types of fastener

Competences:
- describing parts of a nail
- talking about types of nail
- listening to a recording

1 The parts of a nail

A nail consists of different parts. Complete the sentences with words from the diagram.

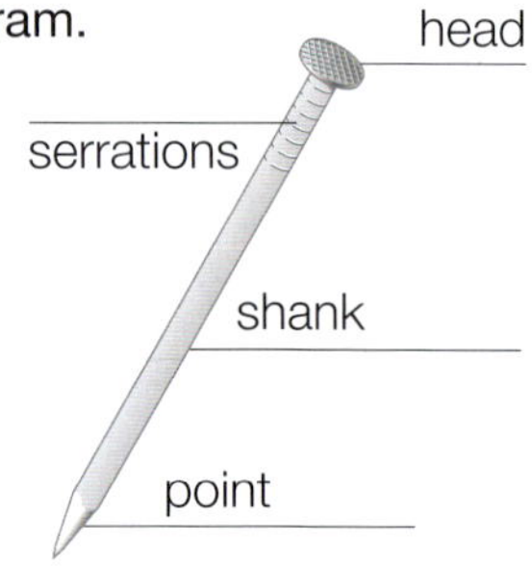

1 The ______________ is struck with a hammer.
2 The ______________ penetrates the wood.
3 The ______________ determines the length and strength of the nail.
4 The ______________ give the nail holding power.

2 Types of nail

As a carpenter, you have to know the different types of nail and what they are used for. Work with a partner to decide what you would use these nails for.

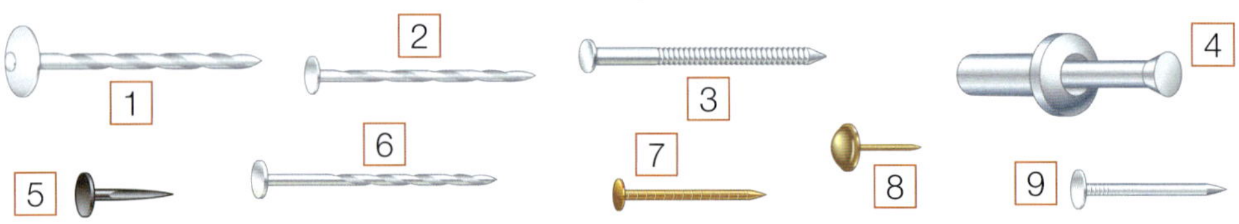

1	Pallet nails	are used for fixing	concrete	to	PVC sheets.
2	Screw nails		metal		doorframes.
3	Clout nails		plywood		rafters.
4	Mortar plugs		plasterboard		floorboards.
5	Upholstery nails		cloth		picture frames.
6	Bronze slating nails		leather		chipboard.
7	Cut tacks		roof tiles		bricks.
8	Stainless-steel stick nails		battens		tarboard.
9	Roofing nails		…		…

3 Types of fastener

Do you know all the different types of fastener? Label the illustrations with words from the box.

biscuit fasteners • bolts • corrugated fasteners • glue • nails • rivets • screws • staples

1

Shutterstock / victoriakh
____

2

Shutterstock / Andrjuss
____

3

Shutterstock / exopixel
____

4

Shutterstock / BW Folsom
____

5

Shutterstock / Margrit Hirsch
____

6

Shutterstock / Winston Link
____

7

Shutterstock / Mr. Suttipon Yakham
____

8

Shutterstock / Charles Brutlag
____

16

4 In a workshop

★ a) Listen to the recording of a carpenter talking to an apprentice in the workshop and take notes. Then answer these questions.

1 What did the carpenter do with the two pieces of timber?

____

2 What did the apprentice find out about "straight" nailing? ______________________

3 What type of nailing held the pieces together more securely?

____

4 What type of fastener did the carpenter use next? ______________________

5 What power tool can you use if you have lots of nailing to do?

____

6 What must first be filled with nails or corrugated fasteners before you can use this tool?

____

7 What safety rule must you follow when you fill this part with nails or fasteners?

____

8 What can happen if you don't use this tool carefully? ______________________

★★ b) Listen to the recording again and complete these sentences with words from the box.

clinched • dangerous • holding power • length • staggering • weapon

1 Skew nailing has good ______________ .

2 The nail gun can be very ______________ and in the wrong hands it can be a deadly ______________ !

3 The ______________ of the nails to be used must be considered.

4 Nails that are too long must be ______________ .

5 The splitting of timber can be avoided by ______________ the nails.

5 At the DIY store

A customer wants to re-upholster an old sofa. He/She asks the assistant for help. Practise this dialogue with a partner.

Customer: Good morning. Can you help me, please?
Assistant: Certainly. What's the problem?
Customer: I want to re-upholster an old sofa. What do I need to fix the material?
Assistant: Is the material cloth or leather?
Customer: It's cloth.
Assistant: For cloth upholstery you'll need cut tacks. They're over here. I'll show you.
Customer: Thanks.

IT'S YOUR TURN

Work with a partner and practise different dialogues. The phrases in the boxes below will help you.

Customer: I want to secure/repair/replace …
- wire fencing / some plasterboard panels
- the back panel of a small cabinet
- a bracket to a concrete wall

Assistant: You'll need …
- wire staples
- steel nails
- panel pins

15 Screws and fixings

This unit is about:
- screws
- hinges

Competences:
- describing screws
- listening to a recording about ordering screws

1 Screws

How much do you know about screws? Look at these screws and complete the sentences below.

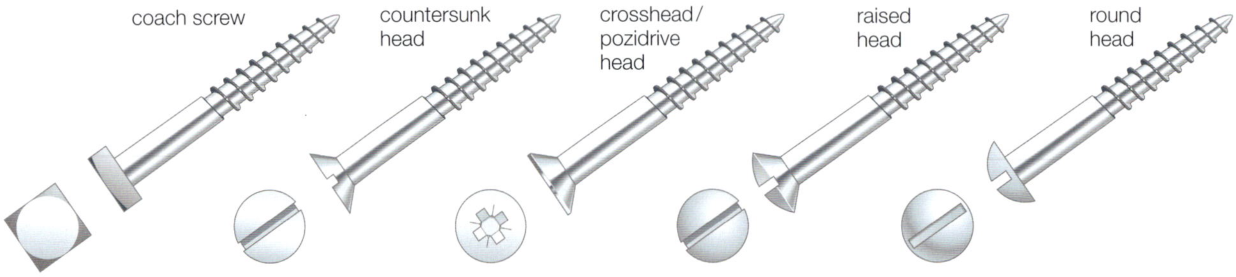

1 If you want a flush surface, use a screw with a ________________ .
2 If you're working with pieces of sheet metal, a screw with a ________________ is best.
3 If it can be visible and decorative, you can use a screw with a ________________ .
4 For fixing things like chipboard, a screw with a ________________ is best.
5 A ________________ is used for securing heavy timber.

17

2 Ordering screws

A carpenter asks his apprentice to order some brass screws.

a) Look at the order form and read the tip box before you listen to the recording.

Tip

Quantity	The number of screws required.
Length	The length of the screw from head to tip.
Number	The diameter of the screw head.
Material	The type of metal used to make the screw.
Type	Raised head, round head, etc.

J. Cavendish & Partner Ltd.
Order Form: Screws

Quantity:	________________	Length:	________________
Number:	________________	Material:	________________
Type:	________________		

b) Listen to the recording and then complete the order form below.

J. Cavendish & Partner Ltd.
Order Form: Screws

Quantity:	________________	Length:	________________
Number:	________________	Material:	________________
Type:	________________		

c) Practise similar dialogues with a partner. Use the order form below and fill it in using the information from your dialogues.

J. Cavendish & Partner Ltd.	
Order Form: Screws	
Quantity: ____________	Length: ____________
Number: ____________	Material: ____________
Type: ____________	

3 Hinges

Read the text and then use the words in orange to label the diagram.

A heavy door might require a pair of butt hinges. Each butt hinge has two leaves connected by a knuckle and a pin around which the leaves can rotate. Each leaf has holes bored to allow screws to pass through to secure the hinge to the door edge and the doorframe. The leaves are sunk into the door's edge and the frame so that the door can fully open and close.

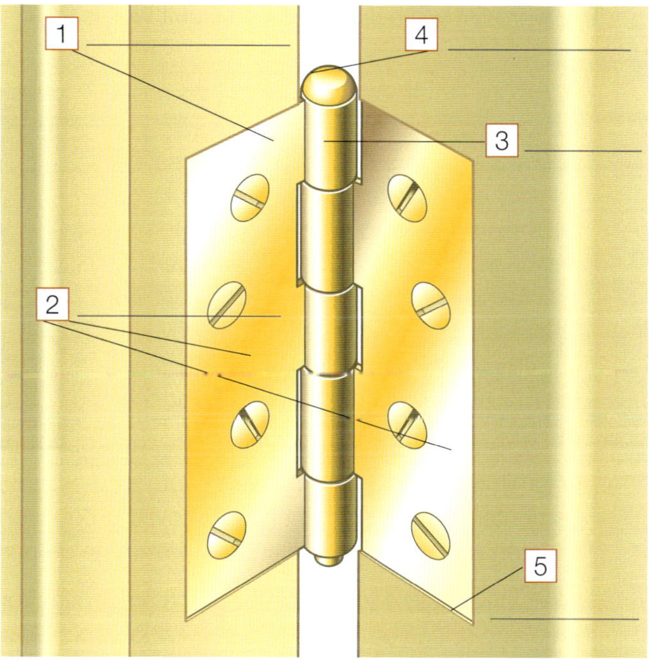

4 Word puzzle

Write down the English equivalents of the German words below. They are all from the unit. Then use the English words to write a short text about screws and fixings.

1	bündig abschließend	____________	6	Oberfläche	____________
2	Verzierung	____________	7	Spanholz	____________
3	Kopf	____________	8	Durchmesser	____________
4	Länge	____________	9	Türrahmen	____________
5	Scharnier	____________	10	Blatt	____________

IT'S YOUR TURN

A customer asks a shop assistant for some advice. He/She wants to buy hinges for a door. Take turns to act out a dialogue. The phrases below will help you or you can look at page 29 for help.

- Can I help you? / Do you need any advice?
- I need … / I'm looking for …
- We have a wide range of …
- What do you want to use the hinge for?
- I would recommend …

16 Computers and woodwork

This unit is about:
- computer control
- computer skills
- emails

Competences:
- describing how to work with a computer
- listening to a recording
- writing an email

1 Computer control

Carpenters have been greatly affected by the introduction of computer-controlled machinery.

Read the text for gist and then put a tick (✓) next to the descriptions below that you think are correct. The word list will help you with difficult words.

Computer-controlled technology has raised worker productivity by allowing one operator to simultaneously tend a greater number of machines. CNC-woodworking machine can be programmed to perform a sequence of operations automatically. This results in great precision and reliability. The machine can now be operated by an unskilled operator – he or she merely starts the machine by pressing a switch and then monitors the automatic operation.

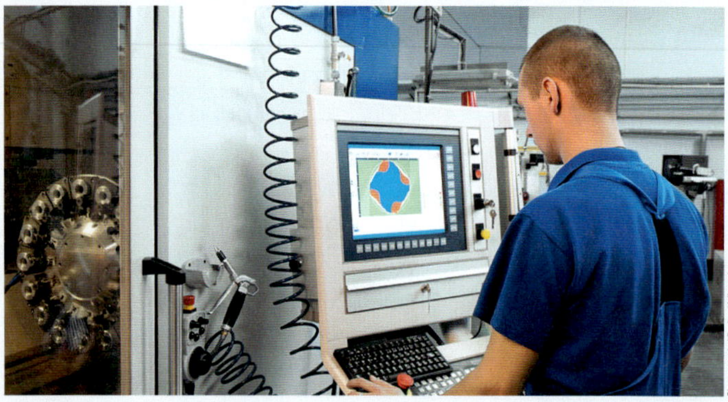

Shutterstock / Dmitry Kalinovsky

In furniture factories, the integration of computers with equipment has improved production speed and capability, simplified set-up and maintenance requirements and increased the demand for workers with computer skills.

While this costly equipment has had a great effect on workers in the largest and most efficient firms, precision or custom woodworkers – who generally work in smaller firms – have continued to employ the same production techniques they have used for many years. These highly skilled craftsmen usually perform a complete cycle of tasks: cutting, shaping and preparing surfaces and assembling prepared parts of complex wood components into a finished product.

1	The text is about:				
A ☐	the work of employees in furniture factories.	B ☐	the advantages of computers in the woodworking industry.	C ☐	how computers have affected the woodworking industry.
2	The first paragraph is about how computers have changed the working lives of:				
A ☐	all woodworkers.	B ☐	unskilled workers in the woodworking industry.	C ☐	skilled workers in the woodworking industry.
3	A CNC-woodworking machine:				
A ☐	can only be operated by a skilled worker.	B ☐	can be programmed by an unskilled worker.	C ☐	can be programmed so that an unskilled worker only needs to watch over it.
4	The second paragraph is about the advantages computers have brought for:				
A ☐	furniture factories.	B ☐	skilled workers in the woodworking industry.	C ☐	workers in furniture factories with computer skills.
5	The third paragraph is about how things have changed very little:				
A ☐	for large woodworking firms.	B ☐	for highly efficient woodworkers.	C ☐	for highly skilled precision woodworkers in small firms.

18

2 Computer skills

Listen to a teacher talking to a student who is worried about his computer skills and then match the sentence parts to form correct sentences.

1 The NVQ is a
2 NVQ means
3 There are
4 In Level 1 the students
5 They must know how to
6 In Level 2 the students
7 They must be able to produce

A learn basic computer skills.
B learn to use a CAD program.
C National Vocational Qualification.
D trade qualification.
E a simple technical drawing.
F five levels of qualification.
G write letters and emails.

1 ____, 2 ____, 3 ____, 4 ____, 5 ____, 6 ____, 7 ____

3 An email

★ a) Link the explanations below to the parts of the email that they describe.

A helen.walsh@eircom.net

B New doors

C Dear Ms Walsh
Thank you for your email enquiry about new doors. I've attached a price list to this email. If you would like to arrange a meeting where we can discuss details, please call the number below or send me an email.
I look forward to hearing from you soon.

Yours sincerely

D Frank W. Murphy
Refit Doors, Youghal, Cork
Tel.: 00353 (0)216 345 116
Mobile: 0187 239 86 09
frankwmurphy@refitdoors.ei

1 The main message with a greeting at the beginning and at the end. ____
2 Your contact information. ____
3 The email address of the person you are writing to. ____
4 Subject: This is what your email is about. ____

★★ b) Write a reply and ask for a meeting. Suggest a date and a time. The phrases in exercise 3a and below will help you.

I think a meeting would be a good idea.	Are you available on *(date)* at *(time)* for a meeting?
Would the *(date)* at *(time)* suit you?	We could meet at …

IT'S YOUR TURN

Discuss the use of computers in the timber technology sector in class. How have computers changed the timber technology sector? When do you need a computer in your job? Are computers useful in your job? Sum up your discussion in a short text.

1 A carpentry firm's website

Many customers use the Internet to find out about a company's services. It is important for a carpentry firm to have a website.

a) Look at the Young Enterprises website with a partner.

1 What services are offered?
2 What services do you think are missing?

Use an online dictionary if you need help with the vocabulary.

Young Enterprises

Home | **Our services** | **Contact us**

Young Enterprises is a London-based carpentry firm.
We have a team of highly-qualified tradespeople meeting customer requests with great care.
We work on building sites but we also do a lot of creative and innovative design work for individual customers.
We cover many aspects of building and associated works.

Our services:

We offer a wide range of services:

- Cutting, shaping and preparing surfaces
- Preparing parts of furniture
- Assembling prepared parts of wood components
- Designing furniture
- Repairing furniture (e.g. re-upholstering sofas)
- Nailing timber
- Fixing chipboards
- Hanging doors

Shutterstock / Robert74

b) Get together in groups of three and imagine you have your own company.

1 What would your website look like?
2 What services would you offer?

Make a design for your website and look for pictures to illustrate the services.

2 Vocabulary project

One of your colleagues has missed class for a few weeks. You want to help her catch up.

a) Collect useful vocabulary from units 13 to 16 with a partner.

Include the following topics:

- health and safety
- nails and fasteners
- screws and fixings
- computers and woodwork

Go on the Internet and find pictures to illustrate the vocabulary.

b) Make up short dialogues to practise the vocabulary. The topics below will help you.

Topic 1	Topic 2	Topic 3
giving safety instructions	talking about nails and fasteners, screws and fixings	discussing computers and woodwork

▶▶▶ ICH KANN

		Seite/Übung
☐	Ich kann eine Rolle in einem Dialog oder einer Simulation übernehmen (z. B. Berufssituation). A2/9	37/5, 38/2c
☐	Ich kann ein Gespräch über mir vertraute Themen beginnen, in Gang halten und beenden. B1/1	41/ It's your turn
☐	Ich kann Sachverhalte (z. B. Arbeit) und Abläufe mir vertrauter Situationen (z. B. berufliche Tätigkeiten) beschreiben. B1/2	36/2
☐	Ich kann einfache Sachtexte (z. B. Beschreibungen, Bedienungsanleitungen, Sicherheitsvorschriften) verstehen, wenn Bilder oder Grafiken den Inhalt unterstützen. A2/3	34/3b; 36/1; 38/1
☐	Ich kann Informationen in verschiedenen längeren Texten oder Textteilen finden, die ich brauche, um eine bestimmte Aufgabe zu lösen. B1/8	34/3a; 39/3; 41/3a
☐	Ich kann Sachtexte verstehen, die einfach und für ein breites Publikum geschrieben sind und in denen es um Themen geht, die mit meinen Interessen oder meinem Fachgebiet in Zusammenhang stehen. B1/3	34/2; 40/1
☐	Ich kann ganz einfache Arbeitsanleitungen in meiner Ausbildung oder in meinem Berufsfeld verstehen. A1/6	34/1
☐	Ich verstehe das wichtigste von Tonaufnahmen, wenn sie aktuelle Ereignisse oder meine Interessen betreffen. B1/5	37/4a
☐	Ich kann kurzen und deutlich gesprochenen Texten auf Tonträgern die wesentlichen Informationen entnehmen, wenn es um vorhersehbare alltägliche oder berufsspezifisch vertraute Dinge geht. A2/3	37/4b; 38/2b; 41/2
☐	Ich kann Interviews, Berichten und Vorträgen in den wesentlichen Punkten folgen. B1/2	35/4
☐	Ich kann einfache private Korrespondenz sowie berufliche Standard-korrespondenz verfassen, z. B. E-Mails. B1/5	41/3b

17 Wood around the house

This unit is about:
- wood in a typical house
- windows
- stairs

Competences:
- describing the wooden parts of a house
- listening to a recording
- making a list

1 Wood in a typical house

Work with a partner. Think of a typical house and make a list in German and English of everything you can think of that is made of wood.

____

____

2 A typical front door

There is an interesting article about front doors in *Carpentry Today*. Read the text and then label the numbered parts of the illustration with the words in orange.

Doors hang on hinges, which are fixed to the doorframe. Many front doors have a glass panel or panels, which let in light. Front doors are secured by one or more locks. A door handle allows the front door to be opened. Front doors come in many styles. For security reasons, most modern front doors have a metal core (steel or hardened aluminium) and are faced with decor panels of wood or plastic.

Shutterstock / David Papazian

Shutterstock / Vadym Zaitsev

Shutterstock / Konzeptm

1 ______________________ 4 ______________________

2 ______________________ 5 ______________________

3 ______________________ 6 ______________________

19 🎧

3 Different doors for different jobs

You work in a DIY store. Listen to four customers asking for advice about doors. Write the name of the customer (from the box) next to the door you would advise them to buy.

Mr Casey • Mrs Kincaid • Mr Leary • Ms Gorman

1
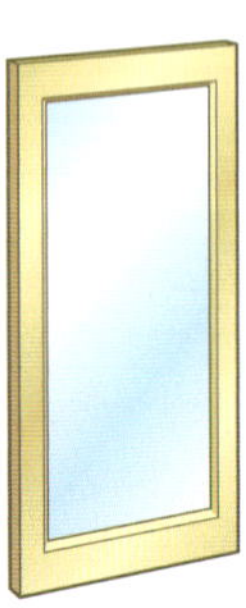

2
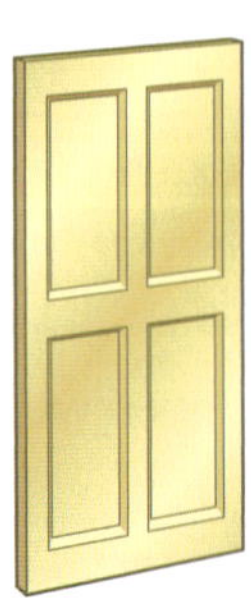

3

4
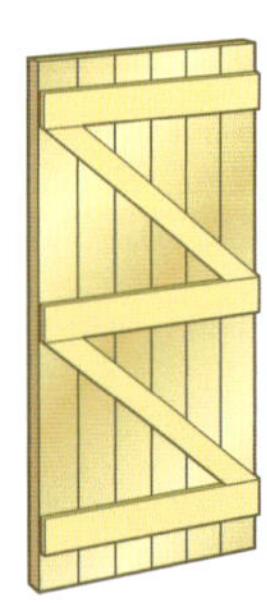

1 glazed door ______________________

2 panel door ______________________

3 flush door ______________________

4 ledged and braced door ______________________

4 Windows

★ a) Look at the illustrations and complete the descriptions below.

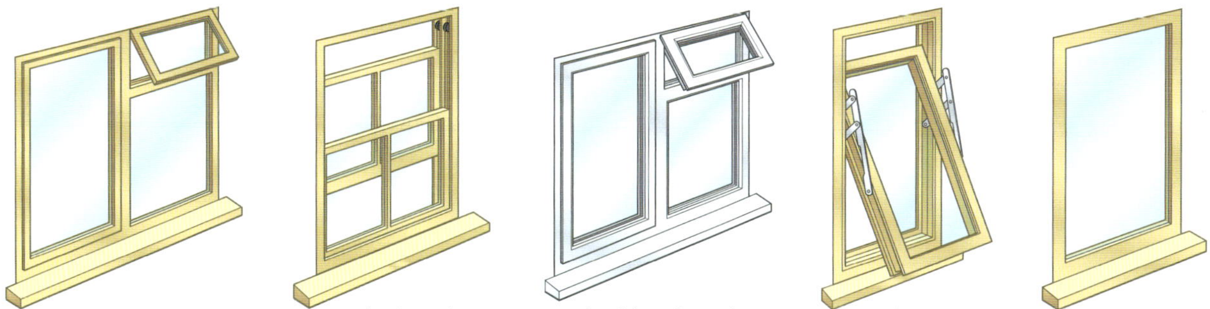

casement | vertical sash | double-glazed | pivot | deadlight

1 The ______________________ window opens outwards.
2 The ______________________ window doesn't open at all.
3 The ______________________ window swings open.
4 The ______________________ window has a double layer of glass.
5 The ______________________ window must be pushed up or pulled down.

★★ b) List the advantages and disadvantages of each type of window with a partner.

5 Stairs

As a carpenter, you have to know the different parts of stairs. Match the words in orange to the correct numbers.

The tread is the horizontal part of a step.
The riser is the vertical part of the step.
The string is the heavy timber that supports the stairs on each side.
The banister provides support when climbing the stairs.
The newel post supports the handrail.
The balusters fill in the gap between the handrail and the string.

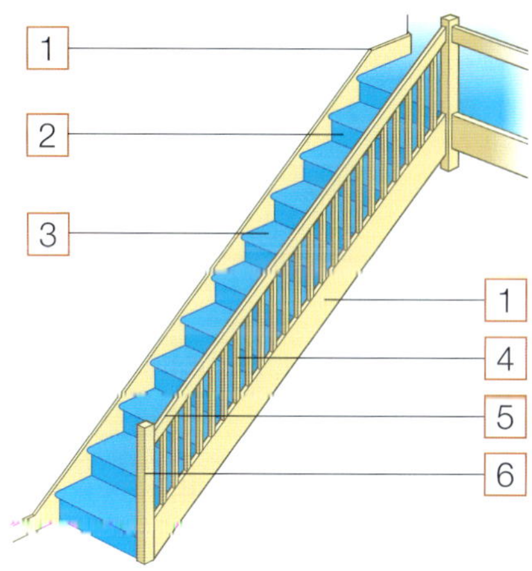

1 ______________________________
2 ______________________________
3 ______________________________
4 ______________________________
5 ______________________________
6 ______________________________

IT'S YOUR TURN
Make a mind map of the most useful words from this unit with a partner. Also include your word collection from exercise 1. Write down ten sentences using these words.

Shutterstock / Olena Rublenko

18 Making furniture

This unit is about:

- furniture
- basic joints
- dimensions

Competences:

- talking about furniture
- making a list
- listening to a recording about dimensions
- writing about basic joints

1 What is furniture?

A piece of furniture – whatever it is – is something which makes life in a house or an office easier. Imagine a house or an office without any furniture at all! There isn't much you can do in an empty room! Every piece of furniture has got a special purpose – we sit on it, stand on it, lie on it, we put things on top of it or we keep things inside it. Wood has been used to make furniture for thousands of years and is still the most popular material for making modern furniture.

★ a) Talk about the furniture in a typical house with a partner.

Student A	Student B
There will probably be cupboards in the kitchen.	There could also be a kitchen table and some chairs.

★★ b) Make a list of the furniture you can find in the different rooms in a house.

Room	Furniture
kitchen	cupboards, table, chairs, …
living room	

★★★ c) Now talk about the furniture in an office and make a list with a partner.

2 Basic joints

Modern furniture looks different from furniture made hundreds or even thousands of years ago, but the way it is made has changed very little. The basic process is still fixing pieces of timber together so that they form a solid construction. This is called a joint. There are different types of joints. The following joints are very old – the Egyptians used the same joints to make furniture 4,000 years ago.

Look at these joints and then complete the descriptions on the next page.

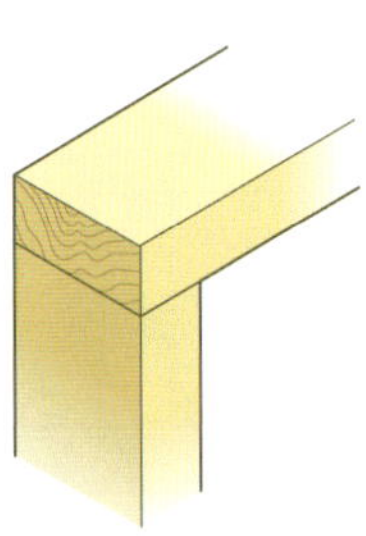
butt joint

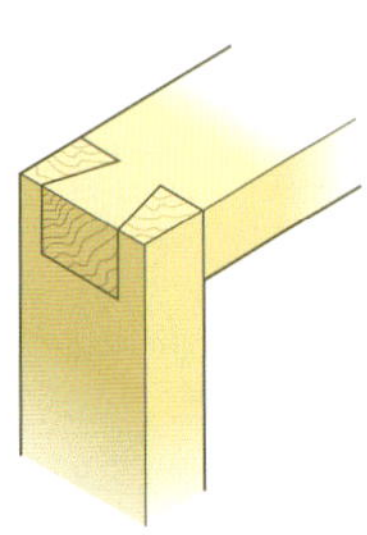
dovetail joint

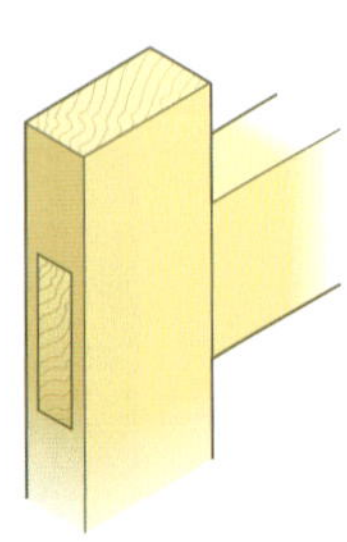
mortise-and-tenon joint

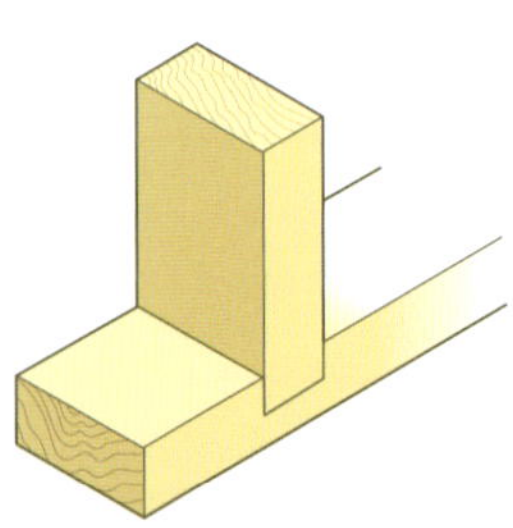
housing joint

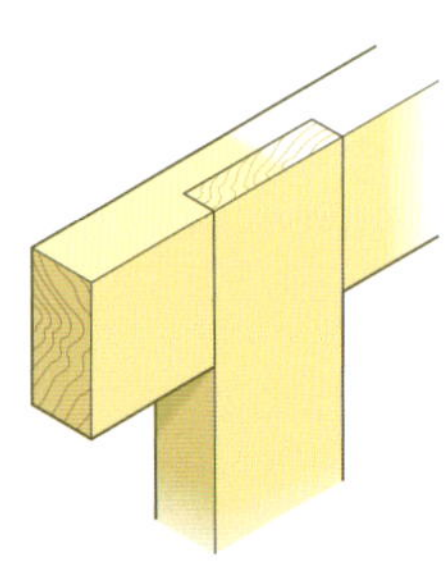
halving joint

1 When the timber is joined end to end to make a right angle, it is called a ________________ joint.

2 When half the thickness of each piece is removed, you can assemble a ________________ joint.

3 You make a ________________ joint by slotting one piece of timber into a groove cut across the width of another piece of timber.

4 If you need a very strong joint, for example for fixing a chair leg to a side rail, you can use a ________________ joint.

5 If you are making a box, you need a joint that won't pull apart easily and also looks decorative. For this the ________________ joint is ideal.

20

3 Dimensions

A carpenter is checking the dimensions of different pieces of furniture.

★ a) Listen carefully and then complete the list below with the missing dimensions.

	Width (metres)	Height (metres)	Depth (metres)
Bookcase	1.75 m	2.10 m	________
Cabinet	0.80 m	________	0.35 m
Toy storage box	________	________	________
Toolbox	________	________	________

★★ b) Now compare your list and your partner's list. Read the dimensions aloud.

★★★ c) Here is a list of materials you will need to make the bookcase from exercise 3a. Work with a partner and listen to the recording again. Make similar lists for the other three objects from the table in exercise 3a.

The bookcase	
Timber boards:	
2 sides	2.10 m × 0.35 m
1 top	1.75 m × 0.35 m
1 back	1.75 m × 2.10 m
5 shelves	1.75 m × 0.35 m
Other parts:	plastic shelf supports

Tip

You write: 0.35 m
You say: oh/zero point three five metres

Tip

nail	Nagel
screw	Schraube
hinge	Scharnier
handle	Bügel, Griff
knob	Knopf, Knauf
castor	Rolle

IT'S YOUR TURN

Make up a dialogue asking for the measurements of the table. Then find further drawings and discuss their measurements.

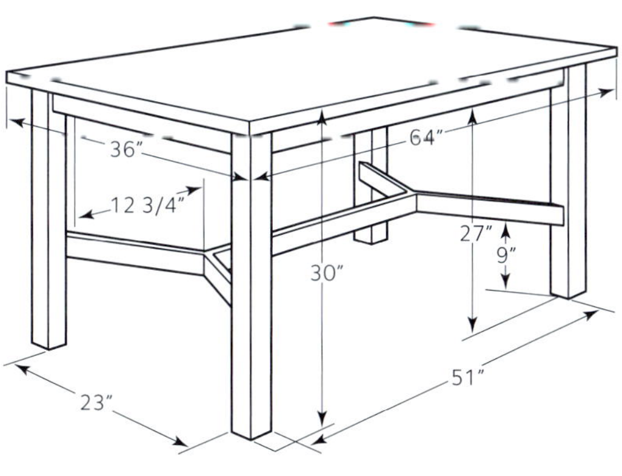

19 Properties of timber

This unit is about:	Competences:
• hardwood and softwood	• describing hardwood and softwood
• strength of timber	• discussing the strength of timber
• physical properties	• writing about timber

1 Hardwood and softwood

There are two main categories of timber: hardwood and softwood. These categories indicate the type of tree the timber comes from and not how hard or soft each type of wood is. Hardwood comes from trees that produce either a fruit or a nut and that have broad, flat leaves which fall off in the autumn. Softwood comes from conifers – these are trees that produce cones. Most of them are evergreens.

Shutterstock / gualtiero boffi

Work with a partner to complete the table with the trees from the box. Is their timber hardwood or softwood?

alder • ash • beech • birch • cedar • cherry • eucalyptus • fir • mahogany • maple • oak • pine • redwood • spruce • teak

Hardwood	Softwood
______________________	______________________
______________________	______________________

2 Strength

How strong is a length of timber? How can you find out? Here are two very simple tests using a plank.

a) Discuss these two tests with a partner. The box below will help you.

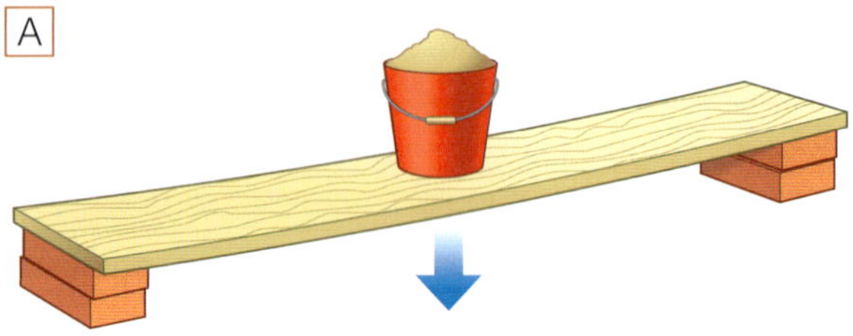

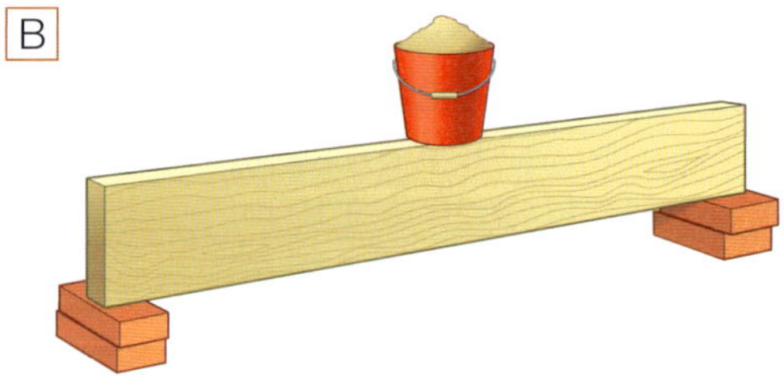

The timber in A will bend more/less than the timber in B.

The harder/softer the timber is, the more/less it will bend.

b) Complete this test report with words from the box.

bend • edge • ends • side • weight

1 The plank is supported at both ________________ .
2 A heavy ________________ is placed in the middle of the plank.
3 The plank will always ________________ more in Test A than in Test B.
4 The plank is always stronger when it is placed on its ________________ .
5 The timber is always weaker when it is placed on its ________________ .

3 Physical properties

Work with a partner. What properties should the timber have for the jobs in the table below? Suggest a suitable type of wood for each object.

Different types of wood have different properties. Harder woods are more suitable than softer woods for bearing heavy loads and tolerating lots of use. However, softer woods are easier to work with and more suitable for carving and turning. Some woods are flexible and will bend under strain, while less flexible woods will simply break. Some woods have very little grain pattern, while other woods such as oak or walnut have very distinctive grains that look attractive when used for furniture. An experienced carpenter should always choose a wood with properties that are suitable for the job.

Jobs	Physical properties					Wood
	strong	hard	soft	flexible	attractive grain	
carport	✓					
window frame						
front door						
bathroom door						
bathroom cabinet						
parquet flooring						
chess set						
coffee table						
office desk						
flute						
guitar						
garden shed						

4 A quiz about wood

★ a) You have learnt a lot about properties of wood in this unit. Decide if these statements are true (✓) or false (✗).

1. Balsa wood is the heaviest type of wood. ______
2. Ash is used for sports equipment and tools. ______
3. Oak can't be bent by steaming it. ______
4. Larch is good for building boats. ______
5. Ebony is a very light-coloured timber. ______
6. Beech is a flexible timber. ______
7. Lime is unsuitable for carving. ______
8. Teak is unsuitable for outdoor chairs. ______
9. Pine is good for cheap boxes. ______
10. Walnut is unsuitable for pipes. ______

★★ b) Write the correct statements in your exercise book.

IT'S YOUR TURN

Make up a dialogue between a carpenter and a customer and act it out in front of the class with a partner. The customer wants to have a new front door and the carpenter gives him/her some advice. Include the following questions: What wood should the customer use? What physical properties should the wood have? The language from units 11, 14 and 15 may help you.

20 Timber and the environment

This unit is about:
- deforestation
- types of legal logging

Competences:
- writing about deforestation
- writing about types of legal logging
- describing furniture

1 Deforestation

The world's remaining forests are rapidly disappearing so companies need to consider the environment when doing business.

★ a) Read the text and then answer the questions below. The word list will help you with difficult words.

The world's remaining forests are rapidly disappearing at a rate of over 23 million acres every year. The cause of most of this destruction is the illegal felling of trees for their timber. This process generally follows the same pattern worldwide. The first phase is gaining illegal access to a forest by building roads through it and then encouraging people to settle there. Then trees are cut down and the timber is removed secretly and without official permits. In the next phase, even rare species of tree are felled, whether these trees are officially protected or not. In the final phase, as many trees as possible are cut down and removed, regardless of any laws which limit the amount of felling. There are several things that could be done to halt and reverse this serious situation. Simply enforcing national and international laws and certifying all timber-processing companies would be a major step forward. A system for tracking timber from source to sale would also be a great help. Such systems are already in operation in some countries.

1 What is the main cause of the disappearance of the world's forests?

____

2 How many acres of forest are being destroyed every year?

____

3 How do illegal logging operations gain access to the forest?

____

4 What is the final phase of an illegal logging operation?

____

5 What two things could limit the amount of illegal logging?

____

★★ b) Decide if these statements are true (T), false (F) or not mentioned in the text (NM).

1 Every year very large areas of forest are destroyed worldwide. ______
2 Legal logging operations are responsible for most of the deforestation. ______
3 There is no obvious pattern to the worldwide process of illegal logging. ______
4 Illegal logging companies simply ignore local and international laws. ______
5 Many local government officials cooperate with illegal logging companies. ______
6 Official permits have proved to be an effective way of controlling illegal logging. ______
7 The trees and plants in a forest are valuable resources for future medicines. ______
8 There is no real solution to the problem of illegal logging. ______
9 The tracking system hasn't been tried out yet. ______

2 Types of legal logging

There are different types of legal logging. Read the text and answer the questions below.

Clearfelling means felling every tree in a small area and it's the cheapest form of logging. Over the years new trees will grow in these man-made clearings so this kind of logging does no permanent or long-term harm to the forest. Unfortunately such small-scale logging can't meet the enormous world demand for timber. Reforestation means replacing the trees which have been felled. International and local laws demand reforestation when larger areas are cleared of trees. This can only be done successfully by planting young trees. Planting seeds or seedlings is ineffective – the forest animals eat the seeds and fast-growing forest plants choke the seedlings. Sustainable logging means felling only selected trees, so that the least amount of harm is caused. This process opens up the forest and allows more young trees to grow to maturity. Small areas are also regularly burned in a controlled way – just as it happens in nature. This type of logging ensures that the forest will exist for future generations.

1 Why isn't clearfelling the solution to saving the world's forests?

____

2 What makes reforestation so expensive?

____

3 Sustainable logging sounds good, but can you see any possible disadvantages? Make a list in your exercise book.

3 All about timber

Look at the texts in exercises 1 and 2 and find words that fit these descriptions.

1 A process in which all the trees in a forest are cut down. ____________
2 The wood from trees that is used in buildings and for furniture. ____________
3 An official document to show that something is legal. ____________
4 A system that can follow the route a product takes. ____________
5 A process in which trees are cut down for their timber. ____________
6 Something that stops a process for a short time. ____________
7 The process of replacing trees that have been cut down. ____________

4 Alternatives

Maybe we can protect exotic timber by using more local wood, for example, a garden chair needn't be made from mahogany. It could be made from larch instead.

★ a) Describe what different objects are made of and why certain materials are used. The words in the boxes below will help you.

table lamp • stool • car dashboard • garden chair • chopsticks • patio table • …	mahogany • teak • ebony • maranti • sapele • rosewood • parana pine • ironwood • balsa oak • pine • walnut • beech • maple • ash • birch • larch • sycamore • …	attractive grain • good colour • strong • easily worked • good texture • easy to carve • less expensive • weatherproof

★★ b) Use the words in the boxes to write a few sentences.
e.g. Larch is strong, weatherproof and also less expensive than mahogany.

IT'S YOUR TURN
Discuss deforestation in class. What are the main causes for deforestation? What can be done to avoid serious consequences? What is your personal opinion? Sum up your discussion in a short text.

Extra practice: Units 17–20

1 Timber and logging

Go on the Internet with a partner and find pictures of and information about different types of timber and different kinds of furniture.

Make a poster showing what types of timber are used for different kinds of furniture. Add useful information from units 17 to 19 to the pictures.

Present your poster in class.

2 Blog entry about deforestation

The local newspaper has asked you to write a blog entry for its online edition. The topic is "Why should we care about deforestation?" Write a short text (100–150 words).

Include the following topics:

- What does deforestation mean?
- Why is it a problem?
- What can be done to avoid it?

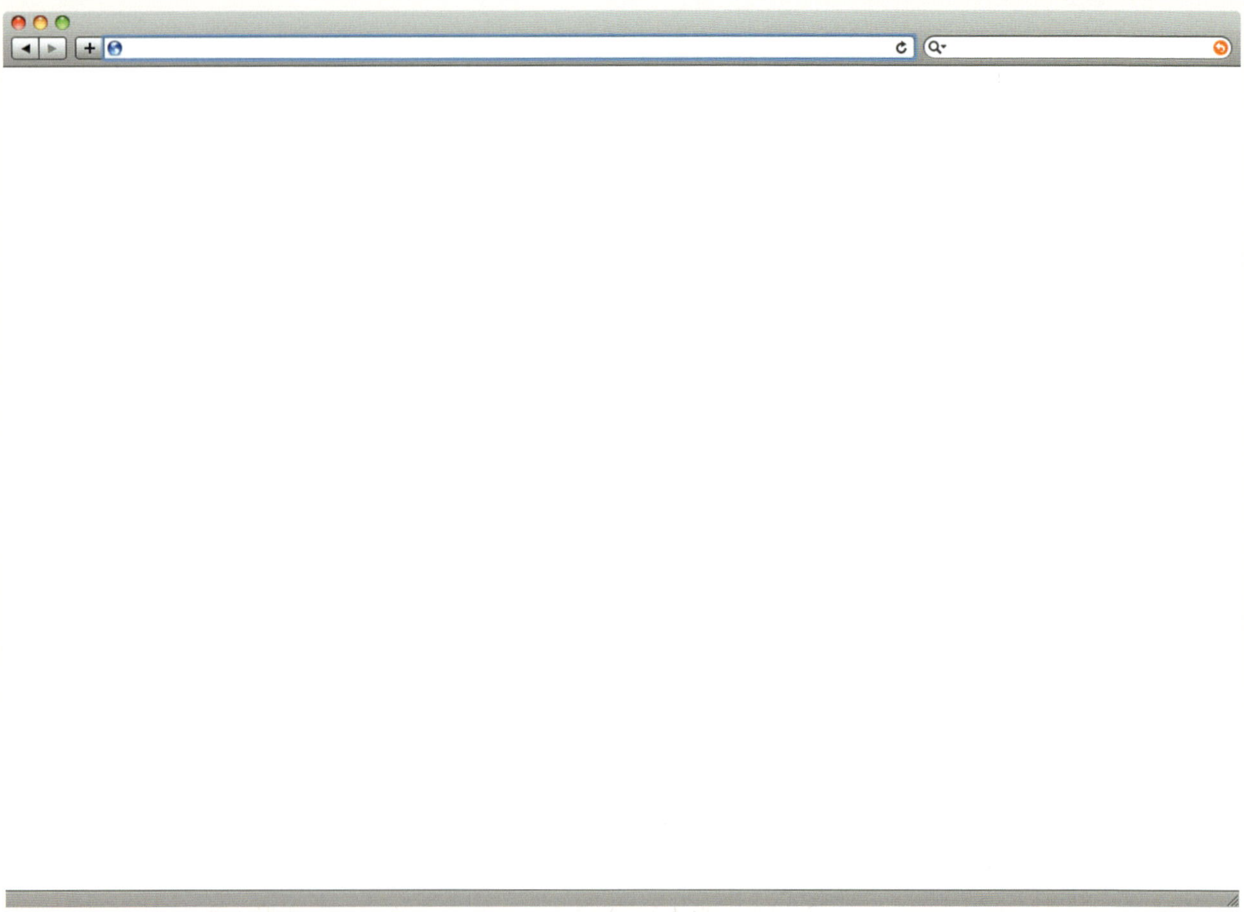

▶▶▶ ICH KANN

		Seite / Übung
	☐ Ich kann eine Rolle in einem Dialog oder einer Simulation übernehmen (z. B. Berufssituation). A2/9	46/1a; 47/ It's your turn
	☐ Ich kann ein Gespräch über mir vertraute Themen beginnen, in Gang halten und beenden. B1/1	45/4b; 48/2a
	☐ Ich kann in einfachen Worten meine Meinung zu einem bestimmten Thema sagen. A2/4	51/ It's your turn
	☐ Ich kann Zahlen wiedergeben. A1/6	47/3b
	☐ Ich kann einfache Sachtexte (z. B. Beschreibungen, Bedienungsanleitungen, Sicherheitsvorschriften) verstehen, wenn Bilder oder Grafiken den Inhalt unterstützen. A2/3	44/2; 45/4a; 47/2
	☐ Ich kann Informationen in verschiedenen längeren Texten oder Textteilen finden, die ich brauche, um eine bestimmte Aufgabe zu lösen. B1/8	45/5; 50/1b; 51/3
	☐ Ich kann Sachtexte verstehen, die einfach und für ein breites Publikum geschrieben sind und in denen es um Themen geht, die mit meinen Interessen oder meinem Fachgebiet in Zusammenhang stehen. B1/3	48/2b; 49/3; 48/2a,
	☐ Ich kann ganz einfache Arbeitsanleitungen in meiner Ausbildung oder in meinem Berufsfeld verstehen. A1/6	48/1; 49/ It's your turn
	☐ Ich verstehe das wichtigste von Tonaufnahmen, wenn sie aktuelle Ereignisse oder meine Interessen betreffen. B1/5	47/3a
	☐ Ich kann kurzen und deutlich gesprochenen Texten auf Tonträgern die wesentlichen Informationen entnehmen, wenn es um vorhersehbare alltägliche oder berufsspezifisch vertraute Dinge geht. A2/3	44/3
	☐ Ich kann Interviews, Berichten und Vorträgen in den wesentlichen Punkten folgen. B1/2	47/3c
	☐ Ich kann Listen schreiben (z. B. Produktlisten) und einfache Formulare ausfüllen. A1/6	44/1; 46/1b
	☐ Ich kann die wichtigsten Inhalte eines Textes zusammenfassen, wenn es sich um Informationen zu einem Thema handelt, das mir vertraut ist, und wenn der Ausgangstext klar strukturiert und nicht zu komplex ist. Dabei kann der Ausgangstext in meiner Muttersprache oder in der Zielsprache verfasst sein. B1/10	50/1a; 51/2
	☐ Ich kann mit Hilfe von vorgegebenen Wörtern, Illustrationen und Filmmaterial eine kurze, einfache Geschichte schreiben oder Vorgänge und Abläufe beschreiben. A2/7	51/4

21 Talking to colleagues

This unit is about:
- talking to colleagues
- communication

Competences:
- talking to colleagues
- writing about professional behaviour

1 Talking to colleagues

main contractor • experienced colleagues • owner • tutor • workmates

Teamwork is an important part of work life. If you work well with your colleagues, the building project will be a success.

Decide which colleague from the box would like you to do the things below.

Shutterstock / Goodluz

Shutterstock / Tyler Olson

1 Who has a lot of first-hand knowledge and expects you to listen to their advice? ____________________

2 Who likes to chat about their private lives? ____________________

3 Who is responsible for overseeing the building work and would like to be treated with respect because of his/her role at work? ____________________

4 Who puts up the money and expects you to work in a professional way? ____________________

5 Who trains you and would like you to follow his/her instructions? ____________________

2 Professional behaviour

Polite phrases	Impolite phrases
Could you possibly be a bit quieter, please? Could you give me the hammer, please? I'm afraid we are quite busy now. Would it be possible to come back in an hour? Would you mind waiting?	Be quiet! Give me the hammer. We are busy. Go away! Come back later. Wait here.

The following statements are taken from conversations among colleagues.

★ a) Compare the following sentences with the phrases above. Mark polite statements with a "P" and impolite statements with an "I". Underline words that express politeness.

____ 1 "I can't hear what you're saying over the noise of the machine, so be quiet."

____ 2 "Could you please wait for a moment?"

____ 3 "I hope you're happy with the result."

____ 4 "Give me the screwdriver at once."

____ 5 "We're taking a lunch break. Go away!"

____ 6 "I'm afraid it's a bit busy right now. Would you mind waiting for ten minutes?"

★★ b) Write down polite versions of the three impolite sentences from part a.

____

____

21 ## 3 Talking about a city's buildings

Markus is a young carpenter from Glasgow. Julia has just finished her apprenticeship as a painter. They meet at an international building site in Berlin.

★ a) Listen to the dialogue and then fill in the missing words.

Shutterstock / Iakov Filimonov

Markus: Hello, I don't think I have seen you at this building site before.

Julia: Hi! My name is Julia and I am a ____________________[1].

Markus: My name is Markus. I am a ____________________[2]. Julia, where are you from?

Julia: I am from Glasgow.

Markus: Oh, that's great. I am from Vienna.

Julia: I like Vienna! There are many interesting buildings in Vienna.

Markus: I also like the buildings in Vienna. Do you like living in Glasgow?

Julia: Yes, it's a very ____________________[3] city. You can do many different things there.

Markus: What are your ____________________[4]?

Julia: Well, I like going to the cinema and ____________________[5] my friends. What do you do in your ____________________[6] time?

Markus: Actually, I love ____________________[7]. I am training to get in shape for a trekking tour to the Great Himalaya trail.

Julia: Wow, that sounds interesting.

Markus: Well, I hope it will be a great adventure. Do you have plans for your ____________________[8]?

Julia: Yes, I want to do a road trip through the US …

Listen again and check your answers.

★★ b) Work with a partner. Read the dialogue, collect ideas for small-talk topics and then try to act out a similar situation.

Nice to meet you.
Beautiful day, isn't it?
It looks like it's going to rain.
Dit you hear about …?
Today I read in the paper …
What do you think of …?
What are your hobbies?
What are your plans for the weekend?

IT'S YOUR TURN

Imagine you have a carpentry firm. How would you recommend dealing with customers and colleagues? Write down five rules of professional behaviour for your company.

22 Dealing with customers

This unit is about:
- talking to customers
- communication

Competences:
- dealing with customers
- writing a reply to a complaint

1 How to deal with customers

On the building site, customers expect polite and professional communication.

★ a) Read through the list of suggestions for successful communication with your customers and then answer the questions below.

- ✓ Greet the customer by name.
- ✓ Be polite at all times and always make the customers feel welcome.
- ✓ Never argue with other members of staff while working on the building site and never argue with the customer.
- ✓ Do not talk to other members of staff while dealing with the customer.
- ✓ Always discuss the customer's requirements.
- ✓ Make sure that the customer is safe.
- ✓ Never smoke or drink alcohol on the building site.
- ✓ Remember that every customer is paying for a service. They should be treated in a polite and friendly way and you should give them the best possible service.

1 How should you greet the customer?

____

2 How should you make the customer feel on the building site?

____

3 What shouldn't you do with other members of staff?

____

4 What should you do with the customer?

____

5 Why should you treat customers with respect?

____

★★ b) Discuss the advice in the picture above in groups. What does it mean? Give examples.

____
____
____
____
____
____
____

★★★ c) Work with a partner. Talk about each other's experiences with customers. Use the phrases from the box below and answer the following questions.

1 How do you greet your customers on the building site / at the office?

____

2 How do you talk to them on the building site / in the office?

____

3 Do you have similar rules in your workplace?

____

In my workplace, we greet customers by their name.
On the building site, we always discuss …
We never smoke or drink alcohol on the building site.
I never argue with my colleagues when a customer is there.
I always try to be polite.

Fotolia.com / Tyler Olson

2 Dealing with a complaint

Your customer has received a table from Peter Young's carpentry firm. The customer is not happy about Peter Young's services and has written a complaint.

There were two problems:

- The table has visible defects on the surface.
- The delivery was one week late.

★ a) Discuss in a group how you would deal with the complaint. Would you offer a reduction/replacement?

★★ b) Write a reply. The phrases in the box will help you.

I am writing to …
Thank you for your letter/email about …
I refer to your letter/email about …
We must apologise for …
Please accept our apologies for …
The cause of / reason for the mistake was …
Since we value your business, we would like to offer you a 10 % discount.
We look forward to doing further business with you.
Yours sincerely

____

____

____

____

____

IT'S YOUR TURN

How do you deal with complaints at your company? Collect ideas with a partner and write a short checklist.

23 Carpentry

This unit is about:
- the carpenter on a building site
- customer service
- the carpenter's workbench

Competences:
- writing about the carpenter on a building site
- listening to a recording
- acting out a role-play

1 The carpenter on a building site

What is the carpenter/joiner doing in these illustrations?

★ a) Write a short description for each picture. The text will help you.

On many building sites in Britain and Ireland a distinction is no longer made between a "carpenter" and a "joiner". A carpenter/joiner's first task on a building site is often marking the outline of the foundations for the new building. This is called "setting out". There are lots of other jobs, too. He/She must make moulds for windowsills. Joists must be trimmed around projections. Rafters must be cut to length. Flooring must be laid and nailed. Doors must be hung. Floor joists must be trimmed and the floorboards must be nailed into position.

1 *The carpenter is fitting / hanging a door.*
2 The soiner is sawing the~~m~~ wooden beam.
3 He is screwing the boards together.
4 ~~He~~ the joiner is glueing the ~~joint~~ joists of the ground.
5 The carpenter is sawing into the joists.
6 He is sawing the joits of the same range.
7 He ~~must~~ is laiding and nailing the floor~~ing~~.
8 The carpenter is nailing the floorboards in the right position.

★★ b) Make a list of your daily tasks and duties and then compare it in a group. How many of you have to do similar tasks?

22

2 Customer service

Three different customers are calling Mr Donahue to make an appointment.

★ a) Listen to the telephone calls and then complete the table below.

Appointments form • Sean Donahue & Partner • Tel. 216 986 104		
Name/Address	Description of work	Day/Time/Address
Mrs Eileen Kelleher		
Mrs Maeve Gallagher		
Mr Eoin Ryan		

★★ b) Make up similar dialogues with a partner using language from the dialogues.

Customer

You want to have a gate made for your garden. You ask the carpenter for an appointment. Suggest a time and date.

Carpentry firm

You are a carpenter and you get a call from a customer who wants to have a new garden gate made. Recommend some material for the gate. You don't have time for an appointment at the suggested time. Recommend an alternative time and date.

3 The carpenter's workbench

Label the carpenter's bench with these terms.

bench stop • front bench vice • tool well • rear timber vice • tool storage drawer

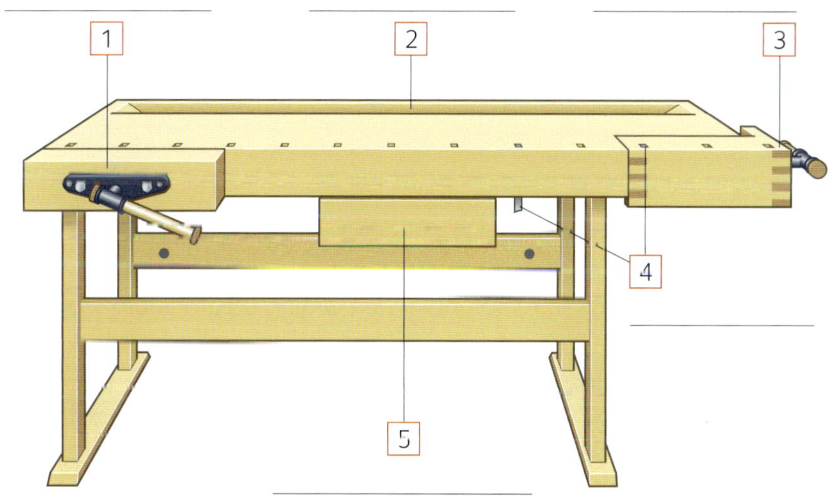

IT'S YOUR TURN

Talk about a carpenter's tasks in groups. Answer the following questions.

1 Which of the tasks in unit 23 have you already performed? Were they easy or hard for you?
2 Which tasks did you like / not like? Why?
3 Sum up your discussion and write a short blog entry.

24 Careers and jobs

This unit is about:	**Competences:**
• on-the-job training • a letter of application • a curriculum vitae	• writing about your training • describing a letter of application • talking about job perspectives

1 On-the-job training and block release

Read the text and then compare your training to Fergus Ryan's training.

Fotolia.com / goodluz8

Fergus Ryan is learning to be a carpenter. He works with his brother Conor, who is a qualified carpenter. Both of them work for a local builder. Fergus learns the basics of measuring and cutting from his brother and other qualified carpenters and joiners in the firm. Fergus must also attend a safety course. When he finishes the course, he'll get a National Vocational Qualification at Level 1. This will allow him to work on any building site in Britain and Ireland.
The block release system in Britain and Ireland allows apprentices like Fergus to take time away from their firms and go to a vocational college for ten weeks. Here the students develop their skills in woodwork, technical drawing and the mathematics they will need for construction work. In Ireland, there's an examination at the end of each course. In Britain, there is a system of continuous assessment during the course. Students then return to their building sites or workshops for further practical experience. This training period for apprentices can last for about four years. At the end of his course, Fergus will become a qualified carpenter. If he wishes to become a foreman or a teacher in a technical college, Fergus can return to a vocational college and then take a woodworking course for a higher NVQ level.

My training	
These things are the same. *I also ...*	**These things are different.** *I don't ...*

2 A curriculum vitae

Here are the most important things to remember when writing a curriculum vitae in English. Read them and then write an outline of your CV.

- List details of your education, training and work experience in reverse order.
- Don't sign and date your curriculum vitae.
- Your curriculum vitae shouldn't be longer than two pages.
- Include any skills and experience you have gained in addition to your formal training.
- Include details of your hobbies and interests.
- The information in your CV should be easy to find: organize it into logical blocks and give each block a heading.
- Don't include copies of qualifications unless you are asked to do so.
- Don't include a photograph of yourself unless you are asked to do so.

Tip

BE = curriculum vitae (CV)
AE = résumé
In an American-style résumé you should also give a simple "career objective". For example: "To obtain a position as a … with a firm in the … area."

3 A letter of application

When you apply for a job, you should always write a short letter of application. A typical letter of application is made up of standard phrases and expressions like the ones in the box below.

What are your skills and motivation for a job? Collect ideas in groups and take notes.

Tip

Use "enclosed" and "enc." when you send your documents by post. Use "attached" when you send your documents by email.

Opening salutation: Dear Sir or Madam / Dear Mr/Ms …
Subject: reference to the job description/number …
Giving information about yourself: I am writing to apply for the post of … I have recently finished my training as a carpenter (NVQ, Level 2) and I am now looking for …
Motivation: I am applying for this post because I would like … I also want to acquire more practical skills in …
Skills: I feel that I am well suited to the post as I am … Moreover, I am sure that my training and work experience will ensure …
Call for action: I look forward to hearing from you soon.
Closing salutation: Yours faithfully/sincerely

4 Job advertisements

These job adverts are from the Internet and local and national newspapers. Read the adverts and take notes.

KITCHEN FITTERS

We are looking for qualified carpenters (NVQ/1) and apprentices with a minimum of two years' training. You will be part of a team that delivers and installs kitchens.
No previous experience necessary.
Salary negotiable. Apply in writing to:
Ms Eileen Quinn, **Kilgallee Kitchens Ltd**,
113 O'Connell Road, Cork

1

Macalpine Construction Company

WANTED:
Qualified carpenters and joiners (NVQ/2) for construction sites in and around Liverpool.
Previous experience of construction work is essential.
Good salary and benefits.

Call: Mr Hiram Fire
(0044) 0151 087 311

2

Type of firm	Job description	Location	Qualification
1 ______	______	______	______
______	______	______	______
2 ______	______	______	______
______	______	______	______

IT'S YOUR TURN

Are you ready to apply for a job abroad? Look at the job advertisements in this unit and discuss with a partner which job you would apply for. Give reasons.

I'd apply for … because …	
I wouldn't apply for … because …	too much travelling / too far away / insecure / demanding / pay too low.
	not enough qualifications/experience.

Extra practice: Units 21–24

1 Application & CV

Are you ready to work abroad? Look at the job advertisement below. Prepare a CV and a letter of application for the job. The phrases in unit 24 may help you. Present your CV and your application letter in class.

Outline of a curriculum vitae	
[Name]	
Personal details	
Name	Jeremy Everyman
Address	19 Clive Close, Sheffield SH4 8AL
Date of birth	5th August, 1998
Telephone number	01143 740 869
Email address	jereveryman@yahoo.co.uk
Education	
Trade qualifications and work experience	
Other skills and interests	
Qualifications	
IT skills	
Hobbies	
Other	
References	
Available on request	

Rainbow Recruitment Waterford
Tel: 051 859880
Fax: 051 859000
Email: wayne@rainbowrecruitment.com
Job title: wood machinist
Salary: negotiable
Job type: Full-time, permanent
Location: Carlow, Ireland
Job reference number: 1645157

Job description:
A manufacturer of furniture and fittings in County Carlow has a vacancy for an experienced CNC Wood Machinist (NVQ, Level 2). You will be responsible for the set-up, programming and operation of CNC machinery in the manufacture of wooden doors, surfaces, panelling, etc.

Candidates should have at least three years of post-apprentice experience in a similar role.

Our client wants to attract candidates of high quality and the salary and conditions they are offering reflect this.

If you would like to know more about this position, please **contact Wayne Mitten (051) 859880** for an informal discussion or email your contact details to the address above.

2 A job interview

You have a job interview at a big company in Dublin. What questions will the employer ask? What questions would you like to ask? Collect as many different questions as possible.

Employer	Employer
What were your responsibilities in your last job? What are your experiences? What is your greatest strength? What is your greatest weakness? Why should we hire you? What major challenges and problems did you face? How did you handle them?	How many people work in the company? How much will I be paid? …

▸▸▸ ICH KANN

	Seite/Übung
☐ Ich kann eine Rolle in einem Dialog oder einer Simulation übernehmen (z. B. Berufssituation). A2/9	55/3b
☐ Ich kann ein Gespräch über mir vertraute Themen beginnen, in Gang halten und beenden. B1/1	56/1b, 57/2a; 61/3
☐ Ich kann meine Ausbildung beziehungsweise meine gegenwärtige oder letzte berufliche Tätigkeit in einfachen Sätzen beschreiben. A2/4	58/1b
☐ Ich kann Sachverhalte (z. B. Arbeit) und Abläufe mir vertrauter Situationen (z. B. berufliche Tätigkeiten) beschreiben. B1/2	57/1c
☐ Ich kann einfache Sachtexte (z. B. Beschreibungen, Bedienungsanleitungen, Sicherheitsvorschriften) verstehen, wenn Bilder oder Grafiken den Inhalt unterstützen. A2/3	57/2a; 60/1; 54/1
☐ Ich kann Informationen in verschiedenen längeren Texten oder Textteilen finden, die ich brauche, um eine bestimmte Aufgabe zu lösen. B1/8	54/2a; 60/1a;
☐ Ich kann Sachtexte verstehen, die einfach und für ein breites Publikum geschrieben sind und in denen es um Themen geht, die mit meinen Interessen oder meinem Fachgebiet in Zusammenhang stehen. B1/3	60/2; 60/3
☐ Ich kann kurzen und deutlich gesprochenen Texten auf Tonträgern die wesentlichen Informationen entnehmen, wenn es um vorhersehbare alltägliche (z. B. Wetterbericht) oder berufsspezifisch vertraute Dinge geht. A2/3	59/2a
☐ Ich kann Interviews, Berichten und Vorträgen in den wesentlichen Punkten folgen. B1/2	55/3a
☐ Ich kann einen kurzen, einfachen Text über ein persönliches Erlebnis oder eine Erfahrung (z. B. in der Ausbildung und im Beruf) schreiben. A2/3	55/2b; 60/1
☐ Ich kann über meine Familie, mein Umfeld, meine Ausbildung und meine gegenwärtige Tätigkeit schreiben. A2/1	55/It's your turn; 58/1a
☐ Ich kann einfache private Korrespondenz sowie berufliche Standardkorrespondenz verfassen, z. B. E-Mail.	57/2b

Wordlist

A	
abroad	*im Ausland*
absolute zero	*absoluter Nullpunkt*
to absorb	*aufnehmen, absorbieren*
access	*Zugang*
to adapt	*(sich) anpassen*
adjustable bevel	*Gehrungsschmiege, Stellwinkel*
adjustable metal cutting saw	*verstellbare Metallsäge*
air circulation	*Luftzirkulation*
alder	*Erle*
angle	*Winkel*
applicant	*Bewerber/in*
appointment	*Termin, Verabredung*
apprentice	*Lehrling, Auszubildende/r*
architect	*Architekt/in*
area	*Fläche*
ash	*Esche*
assembling	*Montieren, Zusammenbau*
assistant	*Verkäufer/in*
axe	*Zimmermannsaxt*
B	
background	*Hintergrund*
ball race	*Freilauf*
balsa	*Balsaholz*
balusters	*Geländersprossen*
bandsaw	*Bandsäge*
bark	*Rinde, Borke*
bathroom cabinet	*Badezimmerschrank*
batten	*Leiste, Latte, Batten*
to bear	*(er)tragen*
beech	*Buche*
beetle	*Käfer*
belt sander	*Bandschleifmaschine*
bench holdfast	*Festhalter, Haltekeil*
bench saw	*Tischkreissäge*
bench stop	*Bankeisen*
to bend	*(sich) biegen*
benefits	*Vergünstigungen*
birch	*Birke*
biscuit fastener	*Lamello*
blade	*Klinge, Hobeleisen, Sägeblatt*
blade guard	*(Spaltkeil mit) Schutzkappe*
block	*Block, Abschnitt*
block release	*Blockunterricht*
board	*Bord, Brett*
boatbuilding	*Bootsbau*
bolt	*Bolzen*
bookcase	*Bücherregal*
bored	*gebohrt*
bowing	*Längsverformung*
bowsaw	*Bügelsäge*
bracket	*Träger*
branch	*Ast, Zweig*
breadth	*Breite*
bronze	*Bronze, Bronze-, bronzefarben*
builder	*Bauarbeiter/in; Baufirma*
building site	*Baustelle*
butt hinge	*Angel-, Scharnierband*
butt joint	*stumpfe Verbindung*
C	
cabinet	*Schränkchen, Schrank*
cabinetmaker	*Möbeltischler/in, -schreiner/in*
cable	*Kabel*
candidate	*Bewerber/in*
capability	*Leistung*
car dashboard	*Armaturenbrett*
carpenter	*Zimmermann, Tischler/in*
carver's mallet	*Fäustel, Klöppel, Schlegel*
carving	*(Holz-)Schnitzerei, Schnitzen, Meißeln*
carving chisel	*Holzschnittbeitel*
casement window	*Flügelfenster*
cast-iron	*gusseisern*
castor	*(Lauf-)Rolle*
category	*Kategorie, Klasse*
C-clamp	*Holzzwinge, Leimknecht*
cedar	*Zeder*
cellulose	*Zellulose*
certification	*Zulassung, Anerkennung*
chainsaw	*Kettensäge*
chamber	*Kammer*
cherry	*Kirsche*
chess set	*Schachspiel*
chipboard	*Spanplatte, -holz*
chisel	*Meißel, Beitel*
chopsticks	*Essstäbchen*
chuck	*(Bohr-)Futter*
circular saw	*Kreissäge*
clearing	*Lichtung*
clinched	*geklammert*
cloth	*Stoff, Tuch*
clothing	*Kleidung*
clout nail	*Blatt-, Schuhnagel*
CNC-woodworking machine	*computergesteuerte Holzbearbeitungsmaschine*
coach screw	*Schlüsselschraube*
coffee table	*Couchtisch*
collar	*Feststell-, Handmutter*
communication skills	*Kommunikationsfähigkeit*
compartment method	*Kammermethode*
competitive	*wettbewerbs-, konkurrenzfähig*
conditions	*Konditionen, Bedingungen*
cone	*Kegel, (Tannen)Zapfen*
conifer	*Nadelbaum*
construction	*Konstruktion*
contrast	*Gegensatz, Kontrast*
control wheel	*Stellrad*
conversion	*Verarbeitung*
conversion table	*Umrechnungstabelle*
co-ordination	*Koordination*
cordless	*ohne Kabel, schnur-, kabellos*
core	*Kern*
corrugated fastener	*Schlaglamelle, Lamellenverbinder*
countersunk screw	*Senk(kopf)schraube*
cover	*(Hirnholz-)Abdeckung*
craftsman	*(Kunst-)Handwerker/in*
cupboard	*Schrank*
cupping	*Rundverformung*
custom woodworker	*Maßtischler/in*
customer	*Kunde/Kundin*
customer service	*Kundendienst*
to cut down	*fällen (Baum)*
to cut off	*unterbrechen, abstellen*
cut tack	*Heftnagel, Zwecke*
cutting	*Schneiden, Sägen*
cutting edge	*Schneide, Schnittkante*
CV (curriculum vitae)	*Lebenslauf*
cycle of tasks	*Reihe von Arbeitsschritten*
D	
to damage	*beschädigen*
damaged	*beschädigt*
dead knot	*Astloch*
deadlight (window)	*feststehendes Fenster*
to decay	*verfaulen, verrotten, vermodern*
decoration	*Verzierung*
decor panel	*Dekorfüllung, -paneel*
defects	*Fehler, Schäden, Defekte*
deforestation	*Abholzung, Entwaldung, (Wald-) Rodung*
to deliver	*ausliefern*
depth	*Tiefe*
destruction	*Zerstörung, Vernichtung*
diameter	*Durchmesser*
dimensioning	*Übertragung von Abmessungen/ Ausmaße*
dimensions	*Abmessungen, Maße*
dining table	*Esstisch*
director	*Geschäftsführer/in*
distinction	*Unterschied, Unterscheidung*

distribution	*Vertrieb, (Aus-) Lieferung*
division	*Abteilung*
DIY store	*Heimwerkergeschäft, Baumarkt*
door handle	*Türklinke, -griff*
doorframe	*Türrahmen, Zarge*
double-glazed window	*Doppelfenster*
dovetail joint	*Zinkverbindung, Schwalben-schwanzverbindung*
drawing	*Zeichnen*
drill	*Bohrer, Bohrmaschine*
driving licence	*Führerschein*

E

ear protectors	*Ohrenschützer*
ebony	*Ebenholz*
efficient	*(leistungs)fähig*
elaborate	*kunstvoll, aufwändig*
electrocution	*(Tod durch) Stromschlag*
enclosure	*Anlage*
end check	*Endriss*
energy	*Energie*
environment	*Umwelt*
equipment	*Ausstattung, Geräte, Einrichtung*
eraser	*Radiergummi*
essential	*(absolut) notwendig, wesentlich*
eucalyptus	*Eukalyptus*
experienced	*erfahren, mit Berufserfahrung*
exposed	*ausgesetzt*
external door	*Außentür*

F

factory	*Fabrik*
fastener	*Heftnagel*
to fell	*fällen (Baum)*
felling	*Fällen*
fence	*Zaun, Anschlaglineal bei Tischkreissäge*
fence post	*Zaunpfahl*
fencing wire	*Zaundraht*
ferrule	*Ringbeschlag, End-, Hirnring*
finished product	*Fertigprodukt, -ware*
fir	*Tanne*
fire	*Feuer, Brand*
firmer chisel	*Stechbeitel*
first aid	*erste Hilfe*
first-aid-station	*Erste-Hilfe-Stelle*
fishing boat	*Fischerboot*
fittings	*Einrichtung, Beschläge*
fixing	*Befestigen*
fixings	*Zubehör*
flexible	*flexibel, biegbar*
floor joist	*Fußbodenträger*
flush (surface)	*glatt, bündig (abschließend)*
flush door	*Türblatt*
flute	*Flöte*
foreman	*Vorarbeiter*
forest	*Wald, Forst*
forester	*Förster/in*
foundations	*Fundamente*
freehand	*freihändig*
frog	*Frosch*
front bench vice	*Vorderzange*
front door	*Eingangs-, Haustür*
fungus (*pl* fungi)	*Pilz*
furniture	*Möbel(stücke)*

G

garden furniture	*Gartenmöbel*
garden shed	*Schuppen*
gate	*Tor, Gatter*
gist	*Kern, Wesentliche(s)*
glass panel	*Glasscheibe*
glazed door	*Rahmentür mit Glas*
glue	*Klebstoff, Leim*
to glue	*verleimen, kleben*
glue gun	*Klebepistole*
grade (pencil)	*Härtegrad*
grain	*Maserung*
green timber	*grünes Holz*
grid	*Gitter, Schema, Tabelle*
ground edge	*geschliffene Schnittkante*
groove	*(Längs-)Nut, Rille, (Hohl-)Kehle*
growth rings	*Jahresringe*
grub	*Larve*

H

hacksaw	*Eisen-, Bügelsäge*
halving joint	*Überplattung*
hammer	*(Zimmermanns-) Hammer*
handle	*(Hand-)Griff*
handrail	*Handlauf*
handsaw	*Handsäge, Fuchs-schwanzsäge*
hand tool	*Handwerkzeug*
hardwood	*Hartholz*
to hatch	*schlüpfen*
hatchet	*Handbeil*
head	*Kopf*
heading	*Überschrift*
health	*Gesundheit*
heavy-duty	*Hochleistungs-, strapazierfähig*
height	*Höhe, Größe*
hinge	*Scharnier, Angel*
holding power	*Festigkeit, Stabilität*
horizontal	*horizontal, waagerecht*
housing joint	*Nutverbindung*

I

inclined	*geneigt, schräg, schief*
inclined plane	*schiefe Ebene*
ineffective	*wirkungslos, ineffektiv*
initiative	*Initiative*
injury	*Verletzung*
insect	*Insekt*
to install	*installieren, einbauen, einrichten*
integration	*Eingliederung, Einsatz*
interior door	*Innentür*
ironwood	*Eisenbaum, -holz*

J

jigsaw	*Dekupier-, Laubsäge, Stichsäge*
joiner	*Tischler/in, Schreiner/in*
joint	*Fuge, Stoß*
joist	*Balken, Träger*

K

keel	*Kiel*
keyhole saw	*Stichsäge*
kiln	*Trockenkammer, Brennofen*
kitchen fitter	*Kücheneinrichter/in, -ausstatter/in*
kitchen table	*Küchentisch*
knob	*(Tür-)Knauf, Knopf*
knuckle	*Gelenk (bei Werkzeug)*

L

to label	*beschriften, kenn-zeichnen*
labour	*Arbeit(skräfte)*
larch	*Lärche*
lathe	*Drechsel-, Drehbank*
layer	*Schicht*
layered	*(aufeinander) geschichtet*
leaf	*Blatt, Flügel*
leather	*Leder*
ledged-and-braced door	*Brettertür mit Riegeln*
length	*Länge*
letter of application	*Bewerbungsschreiben*
lime	*Linde*
live knot	*Ast*
load	*Last, Belastung*
lock	*Schloss*
locking lever	*Feststeller*
log	*(Baum-)Stamm*
logging company	*Holz(einschlag)-firma*
logging operation	*Holzfällen, Abholzen, Rodung*
loose	*lose, weit (geschnitten)*
lumberjack	*Holzfäller*

M

machine	*Automat, Maschine, Gerät*
machinery	*Maschinen(park), Geräte*
mahogany	*Mahagoni*
maintenance	*Wartung*
mallet	*Holzhammer*
maple	*Ahorn*
maranti	*Meranti-Edelholz (aus Asien, als Mahagoni-Ersatz)*
to mark out	*anreißen*
marking gauge	*einfaches Streichmaß*
mass	*Gewicht*
to mature	*(heran-)reifen, auswachsen*
maturity	*Reife, Ausgereiftheit*
to measure	*(ver)messen*
medium density fibreboard (MDF)	*mitteldichte Faserplatte*
metal rod	*Metallstab*
metal sheet	*(Metall-)Blech, Metallplatte*
mitre box	*Gehrungslade*
mitre box saw	*Gehrungssäge*
modelmaking	*Modellbau*
moisture	*Feuchtigkeit*
monitor	*Monitor, Bildschirm*
to monitor	*überwachen, kontrollieren*
mortar plug	*(Beton-)Dübel*
mortise chisel	*Lochbeitel, Stemmmeißel*
mortise gauge	*doppeltes Streichmaß*
mortise-and-tenon joint	*(Schlitz- und) Zapfenverbindung*
mortiser	*Lochstemmer, Zapfenlochschneider, Schwalbenschwanzschneider*
mould	*Sims; Hohlform*
to mould	*formen*
moulding	*Profilleiste*
mulch	*(Rinden-)Mulch*

N

nail	*Nagel*
to nail	*nageln*
nail gun	*Nagler, Nagelpistole*
nailing	*Nageln*
negotiable	*Verhandlungssache*
newel post	*Pfosten*

O

oak	*Eiche*
official permit	*offizielle Genehmigung*
to operate	*bedienen, betätigen*
operator	*Maschinist/in*
orbital sander	*Schmirgelschleifmaschine*
order	*Bestellung*
order form	*Bestellformular*
outline	*Umriss*
overhead	*oben, darüber*

P

pallet nail	*Maschinennagel*
pane of glass	*Glasscheibe*
panel door	*Rahmentür mit Füllungen, Kassettentür*
panel pin	*Schlagschraube*
parana pine	*Brasilkiefer (südamerik. Nadelholz)*
to peel off	*ab-, entrinden, (ab)schälen*
to penetrate	*durchdringen, -bohren*
picture frame	*Bilderrahmen*
pincers	*Kneifzange*
pine	*Kiefer*
pipe	*Pfeife*
pivot window	*Schwingfenster*
plain sawn	*gesägtes Schnittholz*
plane	*Hobel*
planer	*(Tisch-)Hobelmaschine*
plank	*Brett, Bohle, Planke*
plywood	*Sperr-, Schichtholz*
point	*Spitze*
pole	*Pfahl, Stange*
polishing	*Polieren*
portable	*transportabel, tragbar*
portable planer	*elektrischer Handhobel*
power tool	*Akku-, Elektrowerkzeug, -gerät*
pozidrive screw	*Pozidrive-, Kreuzschlitzschraube*
precision	*Genauigkeit, Präzision*
prepared parts	*Fertigteile*
preservative	*Holzschutzmittel*
to prevent	*(ver)hindern, verhüten*
process	*Verfahren(sweise), Prozess, Vorgang*
product	*Produkt, Erzeugnis*
production	*Produktion, Herstellung*
production technique	*Produktionstechnik, -verfahren*
productivity	*Produktivität*
progressive method	*Drehofenmethode*
projection	*Vorsprung, Überhang*
property	*Eigenschaft*
protective clothing	*Schutzkleidung*
protective gloves	*Schutzhandschuhe*

Q

quality control	*Qualitätskontrolle*
quantity	*Menge, Quantität*
quarter sawn	*Radial-, Quartierschnitt*
quick-release lever	*Schnellspannhebel*

R

rafter	*Dachbalken, Sparren*
raised head screw	*Linsenkopfschraube*
range	*Auswahl*
rasp	*Raspel*
ratchet	*Knarre*
ratchet brace	*Bohrknarre, -winde*
rear timber vice	*Hinterzange*
reciprocating saw	*(Elektro-) Säbelsäge*
recruitment	*Einstellung (von Arbeitskräften)*
redwood	*Redwood*
reference	*Referenz, Empfehlungsschreiben*
reforestation	*Aufforstung*
to regenerate	*(sich) regenerieren*
relative (size)	*relativ*
removal	*Entfernen*
rendering	*Schraffur*
to replicate	*wiederholen, kopieren*
requirement	*Bedingung, Erfordernis, Anforderung*
resource	*Ressource*
respirator mask	*Atemschutzmaske*
résumé	*(tabellarischer) Lebenslauf*
to re-upholster	*neu beziehen, aufpolstern*
right angle	*rechter Winkel*
riser	*Trittstufe*
rivet	*Niete*
roofing nail	*Dachpappenstift, Pappnagel*
roof joist	*Dachbalken*
roof tile	*Dachziegel*
root	*Wurzel*
rosewood	*Rosenholz*
rot	*Fäulnis*
to rot	*verrotten, verfaulen, vermodern*
to rotate	*rotieren (lassen)*
round head screw	*Rundkopfschraube*
router	*Oberfräse*
rule	*Vorschrift, Bestimmung*
rustic fencing	*Natureinzäunung*

S

safety	*Sicherheit*
safety boots	*Sicherheitsstiefel*
safety goggles	*Schutzbrille*
safety helmet	*Schutz-, Sicherheitshelm*
safety officer	*Sicherheitsbeauftragte/r*
salary	*Gehalt, Lohn*
sanded	*geschmirgelt, (ab)geschliffen*
sap	*Saft*
sapele	*Sapelli-Mahagoni*
sapling	*Spross, Setzling*
sash	*Schiebefenster*

saw	*Säge*
sawblade	*Sägeblatt*
sawdust	*Sägemehl*
sawmill	*Sägewerk*
saw table	*Sägetisch*
scaffolding	*(Bau-)Gerüst*
screw	*Schraube*
screw nail	*Schraubennagel*
sealed end	*Hirnholz*
seasoning	*Austrocknen, Ablagern*
to secure	*sichern, (be)festigen, festmachen*
seed	*Samen(korn)*
seedling	*Keimling, Sämling*
sequence	*Reihe(nfolge)*
serration	*Zacke*
setting out	*Grundrissplanung, -festlegung*
set-up	*Aufbau, Einrichtung*
shake	*Riss*
shank	*Schaft*
shaping	*Fräsen*
sheet metal	*(Metall-)Blech, Metallplatte*
shelf	*(Regal-)Brett, Regal*
shelf support	*Regalträger*
to shrink	*schrumpfen*
simultaneously	*gleichzeitig*
site management	*Bauaufsicht*
sketching	*Skizzieren, Zeichnen*
skew	*schräg, versetzt*
skilled	*gelernt, ausgebildet, Fach-*
skirting board	*Fuß-, Stoßleiste*
slating nail	*Schieferstift, Schiefernagel*
softwood	*Weichholz*
spacing batten	*Stapelleiste*
to specialise in	*sich spezialisieren auf*
spike	*Stift, Spitze, Bolzen*
spirit level	*Wasserwaage*
split	*Riss*
splitting	*Risse, Zerreißung*
to spoil	*zerstören, schädigen*
spore	*Spore*
to spread	*(sich) ausbreiten*
spruce	*Fichte*
to stack	*stapeln, schichten*
to stagger	*versetzt anordnen, staffeln*
stainless steel	*aus rostfreiem Stahl*
stairs	*Treppe(n)*
staple	*Krampe, Heftklammer*
starch	*Stärke*
steam	*Dampf*
to steam	*mit Dampf behandeln, dämpfen, dampfbiegen*
steaming	*Dämpfen, Dampfbiegen*
stick nail	*Stift(nagel)*
stool	*Hocker, Schemel*
strain	*Belastung*
strangulation	*Erwürgen, Erdrosseln*
strip	*Streifen*
structural engineer	*Bauingenieur/in, Statiker/in*
suitable	*geeignet, passend*
sunk	*versenkt*
supervision	*Aufsicht, Überwachung*
supplier	*Anbieter/in, Lieferant/in*
surface	*Oberfläche*
sustainable logging	*nachhaltige Abholzung*
sweep	*Drehkreis*
to swell	*anschwellen*
sycamore	*Ahorn(holz)*
T	
tang	*(Heft-)Zapfen, Dorn*
tangential sawn	*Pariser Quartier, Tangentialschnitt*
tape measure	*Bandmaß, Messband*
tarboard	*Dachpappe, Teerpappe*
task	*Aufgabe, Arbeit*
teak	*Teakholz*
technical drawing	*technische Zeichnung*
technology	*Technik, Technologie*
temperature	*Temperatur*
tenon joint	*Zapfenverbindung*
thermal unit	*Wärmeeinheit*
thickness	*Dicke, Stärke*
thinning	*Durch-, Ausforsten, Auslichten*
timber	*(Bau-)Holz, Nutzholz, (Holz-) Balken*
tongue	*Spund, Zunge, Feder*
tongue-and-groove floorboard	*Fußbodendiele (mit Nut und Feder)*
toolbox	*Werkzeugkasten, -kiste*
tool handle	*Werkzeug(hand)griff*
tool storage locker	*Werkzeugschrank*
tool well	*Werkzeugbeilage*
toxic	*giftig, toxisch*
toy storage box	*Spielzeugkiste*
traceability	*Zurückverfolgen*
trade qualification	*fachliche Qualifikation*
trail	*Weg, Pfad, Spur*
trammel	*Stangenzirkel*
tread	*Setzstufe*
to treat	*behandeln*
trench	*Furche, Rinne*
to trim	*schneiden, einpassen*
tripping	*Stolpern*
trunk	*(Baum-)Stamm*
try square	*Winkelmaß, Schreiner-, Anschlagwinkel*
tunnel	*Tunnel, Gang*
turning chisel	*Drechselbeitel*
U	
uncluttered	*ordentlich, aufgeräumt*
unskilled	*ungelernt*
unsuitable	*ungeeignet*
to upholster	*polstern*
upholstery nail	*Polsternagel*
V	
veneer	*Furnier*
ventilation	*Lüftung, Belüftung*
vertical	*vertikal, senkrecht*
vertical sash window	*Schiebefenster*
vocational college	*Berufsschule*
volume	*Volumen, Menge*
W	
wall string	*Wange*
walnut	*Walnuss*
to warp	*(sich) werfen, sich verformen*
warping	*Windschief, Propellerholz*
waste	*Abfall(stoffe)*
weatherproof	*wetterfest*
window frame	*Fensterrahmen*
window sill	*Fensterbrett*
wood-boring beetle	*Holzbock(käfer)*
woodchip	*Holzspan*
wood component	*Holzteil*
wood machinist	*Holzmaschinist/in*
wood preservation	*(Holz-)Imprägnierung, Holzschutz*
woodwork	*Werken mit Holz, Holzbearbeitung*
woodworker	*Holzbearbeiter/in, Tischler/in, Schreiner/in, Zimmermann*
woodworker's vice	*Tischler-, Schraubzwinge*
work area	*Arbeitsbereich, -platz*
workbench	*Hobel-, Werkbank*
working sketch	*Arbeitsskizze*
workshop	*Werkstatt, Werkshalle*
workspace	*Arbeitsplatz, -raum*

JOB MATTERS
HOLZTECHNIK

Verfasser:	Thomas Ryan, Roland Reiter
Projektleitung:	Andreas Goebel
Verlagsredaktion:	Verena Reiter, Kari-ann Warnakulasuriya
Umschlaggestaltung:	vitaledesign, Berlin
Layout:	Julia Dresch, Alois Kandler
Technische Umsetzung:	A3 Satzstudio, Oxana Rödel, Absatz DTP-Service, Teltow
Coverfoto:	Shutterstock / Halfpoint
Illustrationen:	Oxford Designers & Illustrators

Erhältlich sind auch:

Handreichungen für den Unterricht als Download	ISBN 978-3-06-451322-8
Audios als Download	ISBN 978-3-06-451323-5

Soweit in diesem Lehrwerk Personen fotografisch abgebildet sind und ihnen von der Redaktion fiktive Namen, Berufe, Dialoge und Ähnliches zugeordnet oder diese Personen in bestimmte Kontexte gesetzt werden, dienen diese Zuordnungen und Darstellungen ausschließlich der Veranschaulichung und dem besseren Verständnis des Inhalts.

www.cornelsen.de

Die Webseiten Dritter, deren Internetadressen in diesem Lehrwerk angegeben sind, wurden vor Drucklegung sorgfältig geprüft. Der Verlag übernimmt keine Gewähr für die Aktualität und den Inhalt dieser Seiten oder solcher, die mit ihnen verlinkt sind.

1. Auflage, 2. Druck 2017

Alle Drucke dieser Auflage sind inhaltlich unverändert und können im Unterricht nebeneinander verwendet werden.

Druck: Athesiadruck GmbH

ISBN 978-3-06-451321-1

PEFC
PEFC/18-31-166

PEFC zertifiziert
Dieses Produkt stammt aus nachhaltig bewirtschafteten Wäldern und kontrollierten Quellen.

www.pefc.de